DEVELOPING *the* LEADER WITHIN YOU

JOHN C. MAXWELL

NEW YORK TIMES BEST-SELLING AUTHOR OF
THE 21 IRREFUTABLE LAWS OF LEADERSHIP

THOMAS NELSON
Since 1798

NASHVILLE   DALLAS   MEXICO CITY   RIO DE JANEIRO

Published in Nashville, TN, by Thomas Nelson. Thomas Nelson is a registered
trademark of Thomas Nelson, Inc.

Thomas Nelson books may be purchased in bulk for educational, business,
fundraising, or sales promotional use. For information, please email
SpecialMarkets@ThomasNelson.com.

Scripture quotations are from the NEW KING JAMES VERSION of the Bible.
Copyright © 1979, 1980, 1982, Thomas Nelson, Inc., Publishers.

Library of Congress Cataloging-in-Publication data

Maxwell, John C.
   Developing the leader within you / John C. Maxwell
      p. cm.
   Includes bibliographical references
   ISBN 13: 978-0-8407-6744-8 (hc)
   ISBN 13: 978-0-7852-6666-2 (Repkg.)
   ISBN 13: 978-0-7852-8112-2 (tp)
      1. Leadership I. Title.
HD57.7.M394 1993 93–2789
658.4'092—dc20 CIP

Printed in the United States of America
12 13 QG 34 33

This book is dedicated to the man I most admire.
A friend whose touch warmed me;
A mentor whose wisdom guided me;
An encourager whose words lifted me;
A leader I love to follow . . .
My father,
Melvin Maxwell

CONTENTS

INTRODUCTION

It was a moment I will never forget. I was lecturing on the subject of leadership, and we had just taken a fifteen-minute break. A man named Bob rushed up to me and said, "You have saved my career! Thank you so much." As he turned to walk away, I stopped him and asked, "How have I 'saved' your career?" He replied, "I'm fifty-three years old and for the last seventeen years I have been in a position that demands leadership. Up until recently I have struggled, acutely aware of my lack of leadership skills and success. Last year I attended your leadership seminar and learned principles that I immediately began applying in my work situation. And it happened. People began to follow my direction—slowly at first, but now quite readily. I had plenty of experience but no expertise. Thanks for making me a leader!"

Testimonials like Bob's have encouraged me to devote much of my time to developing leaders. It is the reason why I hold leadership seminars in the United States and other countries about ten times a year. It is the reason for this book.

What you are about to read is a culmination of skills learned in twenty years of leading people. For more than twenty years I have taught these leadership principles and watched with great satisfaction as men and women have become more effective in leading others. Now I have the opportunity to share them with you.

THE KEY TO SUCCESS IN AN ENDEAVOR IS THE ABILITY TO LEAD OTHERS SUCCESSFULLY

Everything rises and falls on leadership. Whenever I make that statement the listeners are tempted to change it to, "Almost everything rises and falls on leadership." Most people have a desire to look for the exception instead of the desire to become exceptional.

Right now you lead at a certain skill level. For the sake of teaching this principle, let's say that on a scale of 1 to 10, your leadership skills reach the level of 6. This is what I know: The effectiveness of your work will never rise above your ability to lead and influence others. You cannot produce consistently on a level higher than your leadership. In other words, your leadership skills determine the level of your success— and the success of those who work around you.

Recently I read these words in *Newsweek* magazine from the president of Hyatt Hotels: "If there is anything I have learned in my 27 years in the service industry, it is this: 99 percent of all employees want to do a good job. How they perform is simply a reflection of the one for whom they work."[1]

This humorous story underscores the importance of effective leadership: During a sales meeting, the manager was berating the sales staff for their dismally low sales figures. "I've had just about enough of poor performance and excuses," he said. "If you can't do the job, perhaps there are other salespeople out there who would jump at the chance to sell the worthy products that each of you has the privilege to represent." Then, pointing to a newly recruited, retired pro-football player, he said, "If a football team isn't winning, what happens? The players are replaced. Right?"

The question hung heavy for a few seconds; then the ex-football player answered, "Actually, sir, if the whole team was having trouble, we usually got a new coach."[2]

LEADERSHIP CAN BE TAUGHT

Leadership is not an exclusive club for those who were "born with it." The traits that are the raw materials of leadership can be acquired. Link them up with desire and nothing can keep you from becoming a leader. This book will supply the leadership principles. You must supply the desire.

Leonard Ravenhill in "The Last Days Newsletter" tells about a group of tourists who were visiting a picturesque village. As they walked by an old man sitting beside a fence, one tourist asked in a patronizing way, "Were any great men born in this village?"

The old man replied, "Nope, only babies."

Leadership is developed, not discovered. The truly "born leader" will always emerge; but, to stay on top, natural leadership characteristics must be developed. In working with thousands of people desirous of becoming leaders, I have discovered they all fit in one of four categories or levels of leadership:

THE LEADING LEADER:

- is born with leadership qualities.
- has seen leadership modeled throughout life.
- has learned added leadership through training.
- has self-discipline to become a great leader.

Note: Three out of four of these qualities are acquired.

THE LEARNED LEADER:

- has seen leadership modeled most of life.
- has learned leadership through training.
- has self-discipline to be a great leader.

Note: All three qualities are acquired.

THE LATENT LEADER:

- has just recently seen leadership modeled.
- is learning to be a leader through training.

- has self-discipline to become a good leader.

Note: All three qualities are acquired.

THE LIMITED LEADER:

- has little or no exposure to leaders.
- has little or no exposure to leadership training.
- has desire to become a leader.

Note: All three can be acquired.

THERE ARE VERY FEW LEADERSHIP BOOKS; MOST DEAL WITH MANAGEMENT

There seems to be a great deal of confusion over the difference between "leadership" and "management."

John W. Gardner, former Secretary of the U.S. Department of Health, Education, and Welfare, who directed a leadership study project in Washington, D.C., has pinpointed five characteristics that set "leader managers" apart from "run-of-the-mill managers":

1. Leader managers are long-term thinkers who see beyond the day's crisis and the quarterly report.

2. Leader managers' interests in their companies do not stop with the units they head. They want to know how all of the company's departments affect one another, and they are constantly reaching beyond their specific areas of influence.

3. Leader managers put heavy emphasis on vision, values, and motivation.

4. Leader managers have strong political skills to cope with conflicting requirements of multiple constituents.

5. Leader managers don't accept the status quo.[3]

Management is the process of assuring that the program and objectives of the organization are implemented. Leadership, on the other hand, has to do with casting vision and motivating people.

> People don't want to be managed. They want to be lead. Whoever heard of a world manager? World leader, yes. Education leader, yes. Political leader. Religious leader. Scout leader. Community leader. Labor leader. Business leader. Yes. They lead. They don't manage. The carrot always wins over the stick. Ask your horse. You can lead your horse to water, but you can't manage him to drink. If you want to manage somebody, manage yourself. Do that well and you'll be ready to stop managing and start leading.[4]

- Knowing how to do a job is the accomplishment of labor.
- Showing others is the accomplishment of a teacher.
- Making sure the work is done by others is the accomplishment of a manager.
- Inspiring others to do better work is the accomplishment of a leader.

My desire is that you be able to accomplish the work of a leader. This book is dedicated to that goal. While you read this book and begin applying these leadership principles, please be reminded of Bruce Larson. In his book *Wind and Fire*, Larson points out some interesting facts about Sandhill cranes: "These large birds, who fly great distances across continents, have three remarkable qualities. First, they rotate leadership. No one bird stays out in front all the time. Second, they choose leaders who can handle the turbulence. And then, all during the time one bird is leading, the rest are honking their affirmation."

Hopefully you will learn enough about leadership to take your place at the front of the pack. While you are making that attempt, I will be honking affirmation to you with great pride and inner satisfaction.

In every age there comes a time when leadership must come forth to meet the needs of the hour. Therefore, there is no potential leader who does not find his or her time. Read this book and be ready to seize your moment!

—John C. Maxwell

THE DEFINITION OF LEADERSHIP:
INFLUENCE

Everyone talks about it; few understand it. Most people want it; few achieve it. There are over fifty definitions and descriptions of it in my personal files. What is this intriguing subject we call "leadership"?

Perhaps because most of us want to be leaders, we become emotionally involved when trying to define leadership. Or, perhaps because we know one, we try to copy his or her behavior and describe leadership as a personality. Ask ten people to define leadership and you'll probably receive ten different answers. After more than five decades of observing leadership within my family and many years of developing my own leadership potential, I have come to this conclusion: *Leadership is influence.* That's it. Nothing more; nothing less. My favorite leadership proverb is: He who thinketh he leadeth and hath no one following him is only taking a walk.

James C. Georges, of the ParTraining Corporation, said it quite effectively in a recent interview with *Executive Communications*:

> What is leadership? Remove for a moment the moral issues behind it, and there is only one definition: *Leadership is the ability to obtain followers.*

Hitler was a leader and so was Jim Jones. Jesus of Nazareth, Martin Luther King, Jr., Winston Churchill, and John F. Kennedy all were leaders. While their value systems and management abilities were very different, each had followers.

Once you define leadership as the ability to get followers, you work backward from that point of reference to figure out how to lead.[1]

Therein lies the problem. Most people define leadership as the ability to achieve a position, not to get followers. Therefore, they go after a position, rank, or title and, upon their arrival, think they have become a leader. This type of thinking creates two common problems: Those who possess the "status" of leader often experience the frustration of few followers, and those who lack the proper titles may not see themselves as leaders and therefore don't develop their leadership skills.

My goal with this book is to help you accept leadership as influence (that is, the ability to get followers), and then work backward from that point to help you learn how to lead. Each chapter is designed to place in your hand another principle that will assist your leadership development. This first chapter is designed to expand the level of your influence.

INSIGHTS ABOUT INFLUENCE

EVERYONE INFLUENCES SOMEONE

Sociologists tell us that even the most introverted individual will influence ten thousand other people during his or her lifetime! This amazing statistic was shared with me by my associate Tim Elmore. Tim and I concluded that each one of us is both influencing and being influenced by others. That means that all of us are leading in some areas, while in other areas we are being led. No one is excluded from being a leader or a follower. Realizing your potential as a leader is your responsibility. In any given situation with any given group, there is a prominent influencer. Let me illustrate. The mother may be the dominant influencer over a child in the morning before school begins. Mom may choose what to eat and what to wear. The child who is influenced before school may become the influencer of other children once school begins. Dad and Mom may meet at a restaurant for lunch and both be influenced by the waiter, who suggests the house specialty. The time dinner is served in the evening may be set because of either the husband's or wife's work schedule.

The prominent leader of any group is quite easily discovered. Just observe the people as they gather. If an issue is to be decided, who is the person whose opinion seems most valuable? Who is the one others watch the most when the issue is being discussed? Who is the one with whom people quickly agree? Most importantly, who is the one the others follow? Answers to these questions will help you discern who the real leader is in a particular group.

WE NEVER KNOW WHO OR HOW MUCH WE INFLUENCE

The most effective way to understand the power of influence is to think of the times you have been touched by the influence of a person or an event. Big events leave marks on all our lives and memories. For example, ask a couple of people born prior to 1930 what they were doing when they heard that Pearl Harbor had been bombed, and they will describe in detail their feelings and surroundings when they heard the terrible news. Ask someone born before 1955 to describe what he or she was doing when the news that John F. Kennedy had been shot was broadcast. Again, you will find no loss for words. A similar response occurs with the younger generation when asked about the day the *Challenger* blew up. These were big events that touched everyone.

Think also of the little things or people who influenced you in a powerful way. In reflecting on my own life, I think of the influence of a camp I attended as a youth and how it helped determine my career choice. I think of my seventh-grade teacher, Glen Leatherwood . . . the bubble lights on our Christmas tree that gave me the "Christmas feeling" every year . . . the affirming note I received from a professor in college . . . The list is endless. Life consists of influencers who daily find us vulnerable to their impressions and, therefore, have helped mold us into the persons we are. J. R. Miller said it well: "There have been meetings of only a moment which have left impressions for life, for eternity. No one can understand that mysterious thing we call influence . . . yet . . . everyone of us continually exerts influence, either to heal, to bless, to leave marks of beauty; or to wound, to hurt, to poison, to stain other lives."[2]

This truth also sobers me when I realize my influence as a father. A friend gave me a plaque with this poem on it. Now it sits on my desk:

The Little Chap Who Follows Me

A careful man I want to be,
A little fellow follows me;
I do not dare to go astray
For fear he'll go the self-same way.

I cannot once escape his eyes.
Whate'er he sees me do he tries.
Like ME he says he's going to be—
That little chap who follows me.

I must remember as I go
Through summer suns and winter snows,
I am building for the years to be—
That little chap who follows me.

THE BEST INVESTMENT IN THE FUTURE IS A PROPER INFLUENCE TODAY

The issue is not whether you influence someone. What needs to be settled is what kind of an influencer you will be. Will you grow into your leadership skills? In the book *Leaders*, Bennis and Nanus say, "The truth is that leadership opportunities are plentiful and within reach of most people."[3]

You must believe that! The rest of this chapter is committed to helping you make a difference tomorrow by becoming a better leader today.

INFLUENCE IS A SKILL THAT CAN BE DEVELOPED

Robert Dilenschneider, the CEO of Hill and Knowlton, a worldwide public relations agency, is one of the nation's major influence brokers. He skillfully weaves his persuasive magic in the global arena, where governments and megacorporations meet. He wrote a book entitled *Power and Influence*, in which he shares the idea of the "power triangle" to help leaders get ahead. He says, "The three components of this triangle are communication, recognition, and influence. You start to communicate effectively. This leads to recognition and recognition in turn leads to influence."[4]

We can increase our influence and our leadership potential. Out of this conviction I have developed a teaching tool to assist others in understanding their levels of leadership so they can increase their levels of influence (see chart on page 13).

THE FIVE LEVELS OF LEADERSHIP

LEVEL 1: POSITION

This is the basic entry level of leadership. The only influence you have is that which comes with a title. People who stay at this level get into territorial rights, protocol, tradition, and organizational charts. These things are not negative unless they become the basis for authority and influence, but they are poor substitutes for leadership skills.

A person may be "in control" because he has been appointed to a position. In that position he may have authority. But real leadership is more than having authority; it is more than having the technical training and following the proper procedures. Real leadership is being the person others will gladly and confidently follow. A real leader knows the difference between being the boss and being a leader, as illustrated by the following:

The boss drives his workers; the leader coaches them.

The boss depends on authority; the leader on goodwill.

The boss inspires fear; the leader inspires enthusiasm.

The boss says "I"; the leader, "we."

The boss fixes the blame for the breakdown; the leader fixes the breakdown.

The boss knows how it is done; the leader shows how.

The boss says, "Go"; the leader says, "Let's go!"

CHARACTERISTICS OF A "POSITIONAL LEADER"

Security is based on title, not talent. The story is told of a private in World War I who shouted on the battlefield, "Put out that match!" only to find to his chagrin that the offender was General "Black Jack" Pershing. When the private, who feared severe punishment, tried to stammer out his apology, General Pershing patted him on the back and said, "That's all right, son. Just be glad I'm not a second lieutenant." The point should be clear. The higher the person's level of true ability and the resulting influence, the more secure and confident he becomes.

This level is often gained by appointment. All other levels are gained by ability. Leo Durocher was coaching at first base in an exhibition game the Giants were playing at West Point. One noisy cadet kept shouting at Leo and doing his best to upset him.

"Hey, Durocher," he hollered. "How did a little squirt like you get into the major leagues?"

Leo shouted back, "My congressman appointed me!"[5]

People will not follow a positional leader beyond his stated authority. They will only do what they have to do when they are required to do it. Low morale is always present. When the leader lacks confidence, the followers lack commitment. They are like the little boy who was asked by Billy Graham how to find the nearest post office. When the lad told him, Dr. Graham thanked him and said, "If you'll come to the convention center this evening, you can hear me telling everyone how to get to heaven."

"I don't think I'll be there," the boy replied. "You don't even know your way to the post office."

Positional leaders have more difficulty working with volunteers, white-collar workers, and younger people. Volunteers don't have to work in the organization, so there is no monetary leverage that a positional leader can use to make them respond. White-collar workers are used to participating in decision-making and resent dictatorial leadership. Baby boomers in particular are unimpressed with symbols of authority.

Most of us have been taught that leadership is a position. Frustration rises within us when we get out into the real world and find that few people follow us because of our titles. Our joy and success in leading others depend on our abilities to keep climbing the levels of leadership.

LEVEL 2: PERMISSION

Fred Smith says, "Leadership is getting people to work for you when they are not obligated."[6] That will only happen when you climb to the second level of influence. People don't care how much you know until they know how much you care. Leadership begins with the heart, not the head. It flourishes with a meaningful relationship, not more regulation.

Leaders on the "position" level often lead by intimidation. They are like the chickens that Norwegian psychologist T. Schjelderup-Ebbe studied in developing the "pecking order" principle that today is used to describe all types of social gatherings.

Schjelderup-Ebbe found that in any flock one hen usually dominates all the others. She can peck any other without being pecked in return. Second comes a hen that pecks all but the top hen, and the rest are arranged in descending hierarchy, ending in one hapless hen that is pecked by all and can peck no one.

In contrast to this a person on the "permission" level will lead by interrelationships. The agenda is not the pecking order but people development. On this level, time, energy, and focus are placed on the individual's needs and desires. A wonderful illustration of why it's so critical to put people and their needs first is found in the story of Henry Ford in Amitai Etzioni's book, *Modern Organizations*:

> He made a perfect car, the Model T, that ended the need for any other car. He was totally product-oriented. He wanted to fill the world with Model T cars. But when people started coming to him and saying, "Mr. Ford, we'd like a different color car," he remarked, "You can have any color you want as long as it's black." And that's when the decline started.

People who are unable to build solid, lasting relationships will soon discover that they are unable to sustain long, effective leadership. (Chapter 7 of this book, "Developing Your Most Appreciable Asset: People," will deal more extensively with this subject.) Needless to say, you can love people without leading them, but you cannot lead people without loving them.

One day one of my staff members, Dan Reiland, shared an insight with me that I have never forgotten: "If level 1, *Position*, is the door to leadership, then level 2, *Permission*, is the foundation."

Caution! Don't try to skip a level. The most often skipped level is 2, *Permission*. For example, a husband goes from level 1, *Position*, a wedding day title, to level 3, *Production*. He becomes a great provider for the family, but in the process he neglects the essential relationships that hold a family together. The family disintegrates, and so does the husband's business. Relationships involve a process that provides the glue and much of the staying power for long-term, consistent production.

LEVEL 3: PRODUCTION

On this level things begin to happen, good things. Profit increases. Morale is high. Turnover is low. Needs are being met. Goals are being realized. Accompanying this growth is the "big mo"—momentum. Leading and influencing others is fun. Problems are solved with minimum effort. Fresh statistics are shared on a regular basis with the people who undergird the growth of the organization. Everyone is results-oriented. In fact, results are the main reason for the activity.

This is a major difference between levels 2 and 3. On the "relationship" level, people get together just to get together. There is no other objective. On the "results" level, people come together to accomplish a purpose. They like to get together to get together, but they love to get together to accomplish something. In other words, they are results-oriented.

They are like a character played by Jack Nicholson, who, while in a restaurant in a famous scene from the movie *Five Easy Pieces*, is told he cannot get a side order of toast. He comes up with an imaginative solution. First, he orders a chicken salad sandwich on toast. Then he instructs the waitress: "No mayonnaise, but butter . . . and hold the chicken."

One of my favorite stories is about a newly hired traveling salesman who sent his first sales report to the home office. It stunned the brass in the sales department because it was obvious that the new salesman was ignorant! This is what he wrote: "I seen this outfit which they ain't never bot a dim's worth of nothin from us and I sole them some goods. I'm now goin to Chicawgo."

Before the man could be given the heave-ho by the sales manager, along came this letter from Chicago: "I cum hear and sole them haff a millyon."

Fearful if he did, and afraid if he didn't fire the ignorant salesman, the sales manager dumped the problem in the lap of the president. The following morning, the ivory-towered sales department members were amazed to see posted on the bulletin board above the two letters written by the ignorant salesman this memo from the president: "We ben spendin two much time trying to spel instead of trying to sel. Let's watch those sails. I want everybody should read these letters from Gooch who is on the rode doin a grate job for us and you should go out and do like he done."

Obviously, any sales manager would prefer to have a salesman who can both sell and spell. However, many people have produced great results who were not "qualified."

LEVEL 4: PEOPLE DEVELOPMENT

How do you spot a leader? According to Robert Townsend, they come in all sizes, ages, shapes, and conditions. Some are poor administrators, while some are not overly bright. There is a clue: Since some people are mediocre, the true leader can be recognized because somehow his people consistently demonstrate superior performances.

A leader is great, not because of his or her power, but because of his or her ability to empower others. Success without a successor is failure. A worker's main responsibility is developing others to do the work (see chapter 7).

Loyalty to the leader reaches its highest peak when the follower has personally grown through the mentorship of the leader. Note the progression: At level 2, the follower loves the leader; at level 3, the follower admires the leader; at level 4, the follower is loyal to the leader. Why? You win people's hearts by helping them grow personally.

One of the key players on my staff is Sheryl Fleisher. When she first joined the team, she was not a people person. I began to work closely with her until she truly became a people person. Today she successfully develops others. There is a bond of loyalty that Sheryl gives to my leadership, and we both know the reason. My time invested with her brought a positive change. She will never forget what I have done for her. Interestingly, her time invested in the lives of others has greatly helped me. I will never forget what she has done for me, either.

The core of leaders who surround you should all be people you have personally touched or helped to develop in some way. When that happens, love and loyalty will be exhibited by those closest to you and by those who are touched by your key leaders.

There is, however, a potential problem of moving up the levels of influence as a leader and becoming comfortable with the group of people you have developed around you. You may not realize that many new people view you as a "position" leader because you have had no contact with them. The following suggestions will help you become a people developer:

Walk slowly though the crowd. Have some way of keeping in touch with everyone. When I was a pastor, I did this in my congregation of 5,000 by:

- learning names through the pictorial church directory.

- making communication cards available to the congregation and reading the cards as they were turned in (about 250 were received weekly).

- reading every interview form of a membership applicant.

- reading and replying to letters that were sent to me.

- visiting one social event of each Sunday school class each year.

Develop key leaders. I systematically meet with and teach those who are influencers within the organization. They in turn pass on to others what I have given them.

LEVEL 5: PERSONHOOD

Little time will be spent discussing this level, since most of us have not yet arrived at it. Only a lifetime of proven leadership will allow us to sit at level 5 and reap the rewards that are eternally satisfying. I do this—someday I want to sit atop this level. It's achievable.

CLIMBING THE STEPS OF LEADERSHIP

Here are some additional insights on the leadership-levels process:

THE HIGHER YOU GO, THE LONGER IT TAKES

Each time there is a change in your job or you join a new circle of friends, you start on the lowest level and begin to work yourself up the steps.

THE HIGHER YOU GO,
THE HIGHER THE LEVEL OF COMMITMENT

This increase in commitment is a two-way street. Greater commitment is demanded not only from you, but from the other individuals involved. When either the leader or the follower is unwilling to make the sacrifices a new level demands, influence will begin to decrease.

THE HIGHER YOU GO, THE EASIER IT IS TO LEAD

Notice the progression from level 2 through level 4. The focus goes from liking you, to liking what you do for the common interest of all concerned, to liking what you do for them personally. Each level climbed by the leader and the followers adds another reason why people will want to follow.

THE HIGHER YOU GO, THE GREATER THE GROWTH

Growth can only occur when effective change takes place. Change will become easier as you climb the levels of leadership. As you rise, other people will allow and even assist you in making needed changes.

YOU NEVER LEAVE THE BASE LEVEL

Each level stands upon the previous one and will crumble if the lower level is neglected. For example, if you move from a permission (relationships) level to a production (results) level and stop caring for the people who are following you and helping you produce, they might begin to develop a feeling of being used. As you move up in the levels, the deeper and more solid your leadership will be with a person or group of people.

THE FIVE LEVELS OF LEADERSHIP

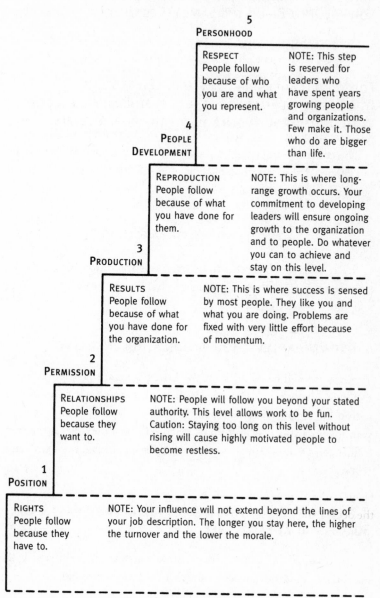

5
PERSONHOOD

RESPECT
People follow because of who you are and what you represent.

NOTE: This step is reserved for leaders who have spent years growing people and organizations. Few make it. Those who do are bigger than life.

4
PEOPLE DEVELOPMENT

REPRODUCTION
People follow because of what you have done for them.

NOTE: This is where long-range growth occurs. Your commitment to developing leaders will ensure ongoing growth to the organization and to people. Do whatever you can to achieve and stay on this level.

3
PRODUCTION

RESULTS
People follow because of what you have done for the organization.

NOTE: This is where success is sensed by most people. They like you and what you are doing. Problems are fixed with very little effort because of momentum.

2
PERMISSION

RELATIONSHIPS
People follow because they want to.

NOTE: People will follow you beyond your stated authority. This level allows work to be fun. Caution: Staying too long on this level without rising will cause highly motivated people to become restless.

1
POSITION

RIGHTS
People follow because they have to.

NOTE: Your influence will not extend beyond the lines of your job description. The longer you stay here, the higher the turnover and the lower the morale.

IF YOU ARE LEADING A GROUP OF PEOPLE, YOU WILL NOT BE ON THE SAME LEVEL WITH EVERYONE

Not every person will respond the same way to your leadership.

FOR YOUR LEADERSHIP TO REMAIN EFFECTIVE, IT IS ESSENTIAL THAT YOU TAKE THE OTHER INFLUENCERS WITHIN THE GROUP WITH YOU TO THE HIGHER LEVELS

The collective influence of you and the other leaders will bring the rest along. If this does not happen, divided interest and loyalty will occur within the group.

CONCLUSIONS OF INFLUENCE

We now have a blueprint to help us understand influence and how to increase it. The blueprint indicates that in order to get to the top, you must do two things:

1. KNOW WHAT LEVEL YOU ARE ON AT THIS MOMENT

Since you will be on different levels with different people, you need to know which people are on which level. If the biggest influencers within the organization are on the highest levels and are supportive of you, then your success in leading others will be attainable. If the best influencers are on the highest levels and not supportive, then problems will soon arise.

2. KNOW AND APPLY THE QUALITIES NEEDED TO BE SUCCESSFUL AT EACH LEVEL

Listed below are some characteristics that must be exhibited with excellence before advancement to the next level is possible.

Level 1: Position/Rights

- Know your job description thoroughly.

- Be aware of the history of the organization.

- Relate the organization's history to the people of the organization (in other words, be a team player).

- Accept responsibility.

- Do your job with consistent excellence.

- Do more than expected.

- Offer creative ideas for change and improvement.

Level 2: Permission/Relationship

- Possess a genuine love for people.

- Make those who work with you more successful.

- See through other people's eyes.

- Love people more than procedures.

- Do "win-win" or don't do it.

- Include others in your journey.

- Deal wisely with difficult people.

Level 3: Production/Results

- Initiate and accept responsibility for growth.

- Develop and follow a statement of purpose.

- Make your job description and energy an integral part of the statement of purpose.

- Develop accountability for results, beginning with yourself.

- Know and do the things that give a high return.
- Communicate the strategy and vision of the organization.
- Become a change agent, and understand timing.
- Make the difficult decisions that will make a difference.

Level 4: People Development/Reproduction

- Realize that people are your most valuable asset.
- Place a priority on developing people.
- Be a model for others to follow.
- Pour your leadership efforts into the top 20 percent of your people.
- Expose key leaders to growth opportunities.
- Be able to attract other winners/producers to the common goal.
- Surround yourself with an inner core that complements your leadership.

Level 5: Personhood/Respect

- Your followers are loyal and sacrificial.
- You have spent years mentoring and molding leaders.
- You have become a statesman/consultant, and are sought out by others.
- Your greatest joy comes from watching others grow and develop.
- You transcend the organization.

Everyone is a leader, because everyone influences someone. Not everyone will become a great leader, but everyone can become a better leader. Now, only two questions must be answered: "Will you unleash your leadership potential?" and "Will you use your leadership skills to better mankind?" This book was written to help you do both.

My Influence

> My life shall touch a dozen lives
> Before this day is done.
> Leave countless marks of good or ill,
> E'er sets the evening sun.
>
> This, the wish I always wish,
> The prayer I always pray;
> Lord, may my life help others' lives
> It touches by the way.[7]

ACTION STEPS TO UNLEASH YOUR LEADERSHIP POTENTIAL

REVIEW:

1. Leadership is _____.

2. The five levels of leadership are:
   (1)_____
   (2)_____
   (3)_____
   (4)_____
   (5)_____

3. What level am I currently on with most people?
   _____

4. What level am I currently on with other influencers?
   _____

RESPOND:

1. List the five top influencers in your organization.

    (a) What level of influence are you on with them?

    (b) What level of influence are they on with others?

2. Spend one hour a month with the top five influencers, individually, building a relationship with them.

3. Spend two hours a month with the top influencers as a group, developing them. Spend one of the two hours reviewing a chapter in this book. Spend the other hour doing a project together that enhances the organization.

4. Review the characteristics of each of the five levels of leadership and pick out three that you are weak in and need to develop.
    (1)
    (2)
    (3)

TWO

THE KEY TO LEADERSHIP:
PRIORITIES

Recently, while attending a conference, I heard a speaker say, "There are two things that are most difficult to get people to do: to think, and to do things in order of importance." He went on to say that these two things are the difference between a professional and an amateur.

I also believe that thinking ahead and prioritizing responsibilities mark the major differences between a leader and a follower, because:

- practical people know how to get what they want.
- philosophers know what they ought to want.
- leaders know how to get what they ought to want.

Success can be defined as *the progressive realization of a predetermined goal*. This definition tells us that the discipline to prioritize and the ability to work toward a stated goal are essential to a leader's success. In fact, I believe they are the key to leadership.

> Success is the progressive realization of a predetermined goal.

Many years ago, while working toward a business degree, I learned about the Pareto Principle. It is commonly called the 20/80 principle. Although I received little information about

The Pareto Principle

20 percent of your priorities will give you 80 percent
of your production
IF
you spend your time, energy, money, and personnel
on the top 20 percent of your priorities.

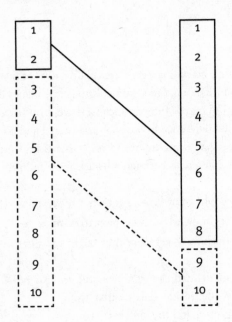

PRIORITIES   PRODUCTION

this principle at the time, I began applying it to my life. Twenty years later I find it a most useful tool for determining priorities for any person's life or for any organization.

THE PARETO PRINCIPLE
THE 20/80 PRINCIPLE

The solid lines on the illustration of the 20/80 Principle on page 20 represent a person or organization that spends time, energy, money, and personnel on the most important priorities. The result is a fourfold return in productivity. The dotted lines represent a person or organization that spends time, energy, money, and personnel on the lesser priorities. The result is a very small return.

EXAMPLES OF THE PARETO PRINCIPLE:

TIME	20 percent of our time produces 80 percent of the results.
COUNSELING	20 percent of the people take up 80 percent of our time.
PRODUCTS	20 percent of the products bring in 80 percent of the profit.
READING	20 percent of the book contains 80 percent of the content.
JOB	20 percent of our work gives us 80 percent of our satisfaction.
SPEECH	20 percent of the presentation produces 80 percent of the impact.
DONATIONS	20 percent of the people will give 80 percent of the money.
LEADERSHIP	20 percent of the people will make 80 percent of the decisions.
PICNIC	20 percent of the people will eat 80 percent of the food!

Every leader needs to understand the Pareto Principle in the area of people oversight and leadership. For example, 20 percent of the people in an organization will be responsible for 80 percent of the company's success. The following strategy will enable a leader to increase the productivity of an organization.

1. Determine which people are the top 20 percent producers.

2. Spend 80 percent of your "people time" with the top 20 percent.

3. Spend 80 percent of your personal developmental dollars on the top 20 percent.

4. Determine what 20 percent of the work gives 80 percent of the return and train an assistant to do the 80 percent less effective work. This "frees up" the producer to do what he/she does best.

5. Ask the top 20 percent to do on-the-job training for the next 20 percent.

Remember, we teach what we know; we reproduce what we are. Like begets like.

I teach this principle at leadership conferences. I am often asked, "How do I identify the top 20 percent influencers/producers in my organization?" I suggest that you make a list of everyone in your company or department. Then ask yourself this question about each individual: "If this person takes a negative action against me or withdraws his or her support from me, what will the impact likely be?" If you won't be able to function, then put a check mark next to that name. If the person can help you or hurt you, but cannot make or break you in terms of your ability to get important things done, then don't put a check mark next to that name. When you get through making the check marks, you will have marked between 15 and 20 percent of the names. Those are the vital relationships that need to be developed and given the proper amount of resources needed to grow the organization.

> Efficiency is the foundation for survival. Effectiveness is the foundation for success.

IT's NOT HOW HARD YOU WORK; IT's HOW SMART YOU WORK

A man was told that if he worked the very hardest he could he would become rich. The hardest work he knew was digging holes, so he set about digging great holes in his backyard. He didn't get rich; he only got a backache. He worked hard but he worked without any priorities.

ORGANIZE OR AGONIZE

The ability to juggle three or four high-priority projects successfully is a must for every leader. A life in which anything goes will ultimately be a life in which nothing goes.

Prioritize Assignments

High Importance/High Urgency: Tackle these projects first.

High Importance/Low Urgency: Set deadlines for completion, and get these projects worked into your daily routine.

Low Importance/High Urgency: Find quick, efficient ways to get this work done without much personal involvement. If possible, delegate it to a "can do" assistant.

Low Importance/Low Urgency: This is busy or repetitious work, such as filing. Stack it up and do it in half-hour segments every week; get somebody else to do it; or don't do it at all. Before putting off until tomorrow something you can do today, study it clearly. Maybe you can postpone it indefinitely.

PARETO

DATE_____

PHONE CALLS TO MAKE	COMP	PERSONAL NOTES	COMP
1._____	☐	1._____	☐
2._____	☐	2._____	☐
3._____	☐	3._____	☐
4._____	☐	4._____	☐

20/80 TIME

ORDER OF
PRIORITY TIME ALLOWED DESCRIPTION—LIST OF THINGS TO DO <u>NOW</u> COMPLETED
(HIGH IMPORTANCE; HIGH URGENCY)

1._____ ☐
2._____ ☐
3._____ ☐
4._____ ☐
5._____ ☐
6._____ ☐
7._____ ☐
8._____ ☐
9._____ ☐
10._____ ☐

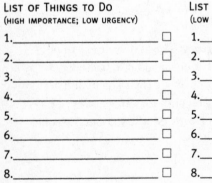

LIST OF THINGS TO DO
(HIGH IMPORTANCE; LOW URGENCY)

1._____ ☐
2._____ ☐
3._____ ☐
4._____ ☐
5._____ ☐
6._____ ☐
7._____ ☐
8._____ ☐

LIST OF THINGS TO DELEGATE
(LOW IMPORTANCE; HIGH URGENCY)

1._____ ☐
2._____ ☐
3._____ ☐
4._____ ☐
5._____ ☐
6._____ ☐
7._____ ☐
8._____ ☐

A few years ago I was teaching the 20/80 principle at a conference in Boston. A few weeks later my friend, John Bowen, sent me a tablet of paper that he designed from the lecture. I have used it for my own prioritizing ever since. Perhaps it will have value to you, too (see page 24).

CHOOSE OR LOSE

Every person is either an initiator or a reactor when it comes to planning. An example is our calendar. The question is not, "Will my calendar be full?" but "Who will fill my calendar?" If we are leaders of others, the question is not, "Will I see people?" but "Who will I see?" My observation is that leaders tend to initiate, and followers tend to react. Note the difference.

LEADERS	FOLLOWERS
Initiate	React
Lead; pick up phone and make contact	Listen; wait for phone to ring
Spend time planning; anticipate problems	Spend time living day-to-day; react to problems
Invest time with people	Spend time with people
Fill the calendar by priorities	Fill the calendar by requests

EVALUATE OR STALEMATE

A veteran of many years of decision making gave me this short, simple advice: Decide what to do and do it; decide what not to do and don't do it. Evaluation of priorities, however, is not quite that simple. Many times they are not black or white, but many tones of gray. I have found that the last thing one knows is what to put first.

The following questions will assist your prioritization process:

What is required of me? A leader can give up anything except final responsibility. The question that must always be answered before accepting a new job is, "What is required of me?" In other words, what do I have to do that no one but me can do? Whatever those things are, they must be put high on the priority list. Failure to do them will cause you to be among the unemployed. There will be many responsibilities of the levels under your position, but only a few that require you to be the one and only one who can do them. Distinguish between what you have to do and what can be delegated to someone else.

Take a minute and list what is required of you in your job (by priority, if possible).

1.

2.

3.

4.

What gives me the greatest return? The effort expended should approximate the results expected. A question I must continually ask myself is, "Am I doing what I do best and receiving a good return for the organization?" There are three common problems in many organizations.

- Abuse: too few employees are doing too much.
- Disuse: too many employees are doing too little.
- Misuse: too many employees are doing the wrong things.

Bo Jackson played defensive end for his high school football team. He was good, but he didn't lead his team to a championship. In fact, they finished the season with three wins and seven losses. At Auburn University, when all three running backs were injured, Bo's coach asked him to fill in "until the regulars are healthy again." Bo was apprehensive, but he did it. The rest is history. This is an excellent example of fulfilling the "return" questions.

Take a minute and list what gives you the greatest return on your job.

1.

2.

3.

4.

What is most rewarding? Life is too short not to be fun. Our best work takes place when we enjoy it. Some time ago I spoke at a leaders' conference where I attempted to teach this principle. The title of my lecture was "Take This Job and Love It." I encouraged the audience to find something they liked to do so much that they would gladly do it for nothing. Then I suggested they learn to do it so well that people would be happy to pay them for it. Andy Granatelli said that when you are making a success of something, it's not work. It's a way of life. You enjoy yourself because you are making your contribution to the world. I believe that! Take a minute and write down what is most satisfying in your job.

1.

2.

3.

4.

Success in your work will be greatly increased if the 3 R's (Requirements/Return/Reward) are similar. In other words, if the requirements of my job are the same as my strengths that give me the highest return, and doing those things brings me great pleasure, then I will be successful if I act on my priorities.

PRIORITY PRINCIPLES

PRIORITIES NEVER "STAY PUT"

Priorities continually shift and demand attention. H. Ross Perot said, "Anything that is excellent or praiseworthy moment-by-moment on the cutting edge must be constantly fought for." Well-placed priorities always sit on "the edge."

To keep priorities in place, do the following:

- Evaluate: Every month review the 3 R's (Requirements/Return/ Reward).

- Eliminate: Ask yourself, "What am I doing that can be done by someone else?"

- Estimate: What are the top projects you are doing this month, and how long will they take?

YOU CANNOT OVERESTIMATE THE UNIMPORTANCE OF PRACTICALLY EVERYTHING

I love this principle. It's a little exaggerated but needs to be said. William James said that the art of being wise is the "art of knowing what to overlook." The petty and the mundane steal much of our time. Too many of us are living for the wrong things.

> You cannot overestimate the unimportance of practically everything.

Dr. Anthony Campolo tells about a sociological study in which fifty people over the age of ninety-five were asked one question: "If you could live your life over again, what would you do differently?" It was an open-ended question, and a multiplicity of answers constantly reemerged and dominated the results of the study. These were three answers:

- If I had it to do over again, I would reflect more.
- If I had it to do over again, I would risk more.

- If I had it to do over again, I would do more things that would live on after I am dead.

A young concert violinist was asked the secret of her success. She replied, "Planned neglect." Then she explained, "When I was in school, there were many things that demanded my time. When I went to my room after breakfast, I made my bed, straightened the room, dusted the floor, and did whatever else came to my attention. Then I hurried to my violin practice. I found I wasn't progressing as I thought I should, so I reversed things. Until my practice period was completed, I deliberately neglected everything else. That program of planned neglect, I believe, accounts for my success."[1]

THE GOOD IS THE ENEMY OF THE BEST

Most people can prioritize when faced with a right-or-wrong issue. The challenge arises when we are faced with two good choices. Now what should we do? What if both choices fall comfortably into the requirements, return, and reward of our work?

How to Break the Tie Between Two Good Options

- Ask your overseer or coworkers their preference.
- Can one of the options be handled by someone else? If so, pass it on and work on the one only you can do.
- Which option would be of more benefit to the customer? Too many times we are like the merchant who was so intent on trying to keep the store clean that he would never unlock the front door. The real reason for running the store is to have customers come in, not to clean it up!
- Make your decision based on the purpose of the organization.

A lighthouse keeper who worked on a rocky stretch of coastline received his new supply of oil once a month to keep the light burning.

Not being far from shore, he had frequent guests. One night a woman from the village begged some oil to keep her family warm. Another time a father asked for some to use in his lamp. Another needed some to lubricate a wheel. Since all the requests seemed legitimate, the lighthouse keeper tried to please everyone and grant the requests of all. Toward the end of the month he noticed the supply of oil was very low. Soon it was gone, and the beacon went out. That night several ships were wrecked and lives were lost. When the authorities investigated, the man was very repentant. To his excuses and pleading, their reply was, "You were given oil for one purpose—to keep that light burning!"

YOU CAN'T HAVE IT ALL

When my son, Joel Porter, was younger, every time we entered a store, I would say to him, "You can't have it all." Like many people, he had a hard time eliminating things in his life. Ninety-five percent of achieving anything is knowing what you want. Many years ago I read this poem by William H. Hinson:

> He who seeks one thing, and but one,
> May hope to achieve it before life is done.
> But he who seeks all things wherever he goes
> Must reap around him in whatever he sows
> A harvest of barren regret.

A group of people were preparing for an ascent to the top of Mont Blanc in the Alps in France. On the evening before the climb, a French guide outlined the main prerequisite for success. He said, "To reach the top, you must carry only equipment necessary for climbing. You must leave behind all unnecessary accessories. It's a difficult climb."

A young Englishman disagreed and the next morning showed up with a rather heavy, brightly colored blanket; some large pieces of cheese; a bottle of wine; a couple of cameras with several lenses hanging around his neck; and some bars of chocolate. The guide said, "You'll never make it with that. You can only take the bare necessities to make the climb."

But strong-willed as he was, the Englishman set off on his own in front of the group to prove to them he could do it. The group then followed under the direction of the guide, each one carrying just the bare necessities. On the way up to the summit of Mont Blanc, they began to notice certain things someone had left along the way. First, they encountered a brightly colored blanket, then some pieces of cheese, a bottle of wine, camera equipment, and some chocolate bars. Finally when they reached the top, they discovered the Englishman. Wisely, along the way he had jettisoned everything unnecessary.

TOO MANY PRIORITIES PARALYZE US

Every one of us has looked at our desks filled with memos and papers, heard the phone ringing, and watched the door open all at the same time! Remember the "frozen feeling" that came over you?

William H. Hinson tells us why animal trainers carry a stool when they go into a cage of lions. They have their whips, of course, and their pistols are at their sides. But invariably they also carry a stool. Hinson says it is the most important tool of the trainer. He holds the stool by the back and thrusts the legs toward the face of the wild animal. Those who know maintain that the animal tries to focus on all four legs at once. In the attempt to focus on all four, a kind of paralysis overwhelms the animal, and it becomes tame, weak, and disabled because its attention is fragmented. (Now we will have more empathy for the lions.)

One day, Sheryl, one of our most productive staff members, came to see me. She looked exhausted. I learned that she was overloaded. Her "to do" list was getting too long. I asked her to list all her projects. We prioritized them together. I can still see the look of relief on her face as the load began to lift.

If you are overloaded with work, list the priorities on a separate sheet of paper before you take it to your boss and see what he will choose as the priorities.

The last of each month, I plan and lay out my priorities for the next month. I sit down with Barbara, my assistant, and have her place those projects on the calendar. She handles hundreds of things for me on a monthly basis. However, when something is of High Importance/High Urgency, I communicate that to her so it will be placed above other things. All true leaders have learned to say no to the good in order to say yes to the best.

WHEN LITTLE PRIORITIES DEMAND
TOO MUCH OF US, BIG PROBLEMS ARISE

Robert J. McKain said, "The reason most major goals are not achieved is that we spend our time doing second things first."

Some years ago a headline told of three hundred whales that suddenly died. The whales were pursuing sardines and found themselves marooned in a bay. Frederick Broan Harris commented, "The small fish lured the sea giants to their death . . . They came to their violent demise by chasing small ends, by prostituting vast powers for insignificant goals."[2]

Often the little things in life trip us up. A tragic example is an Eastern Airlines jumbo jet that crashed in the Everglades of Florida. The plane was the now-famous Flight 401, bound from New York to Miami with a heavy load of holiday passengers. As the plane approached the Miami airport for its landing, the light that indicates proper deployment of the landing gear failed to light. The plane flew in a large, looping circle over the swamps of the Everglades while the cockpit crew checked to see if the gear actually had not deployed, or if instead the bulb in the signal light was defective.

When the flight engineer tried to remove the lightbulb, it wouldn't budge, and the other members of the crew tried to help him. As they struggled with the bulb, no one noticed the aircraft was losing altitude, and the plane simply flew right into the swamp. Dozens of people were killed in the crash. While an experienced crew of high-priced pilots fiddled with a seventy-five-cent lightbulb, the plane with its passengers flew right into the ground.

TIME DEADLINES AND EMERGENCIES
FORCE US TO PRIORITIZE

We find this in Parkinson's Law: If you have only one letter to write, it will take all day to do it. If you have twenty letters to write, you'll get them done in one day.

When is our most efficient time in our work? The week before vacation! Why can't we always run our lives the way we do the week before we leave the office: making decisions, cleaning off the desk, returning calls? Under normal conditions, we are efficient (doing things right). When time pressure mounts or emergencies arise, we become effective (doing the right things). Efficiency is the foundation for survival. Effectiveness is the foundation of success.

On the night of April 14, 1912, the great ocean liner, the *Titanic*, crashed into an iceberg in the Atlantic and sank, causing great loss of life. One of the most curious stories to come from the disaster was of a woman who had a place in one of the lifeboats.

She asked if she could return to her stateroom for something and was given just three minutes. As she hurried through the corridors, she stepped over money and precious gems littering the floor, where they had been dropped in haste. In her own stateroom she ignored her own jewelry, and instead grabbed three oranges. Then she quickly returned to her place in the boat.

Just hours earlier it would have been ludicrous to think she would have accepted a crate of oranges in exchange for even one small diamond, but circumstances had suddenly transformed all the values aboard the ship. The emergency had clarified her priorities.

TOO OFTEN WE LEARN TOO LATE WHAT IS REALLY IMPORTANT

We are like the family that had become fed up with the noise and traffic of the city and decided to move to the country and try life in the wide open spaces. Intending to raise cattle, they bought a Western ranch. Some friends came to visit a month later and asked them what they had named the ranch. The father said, "Well, I wanted to call it the Flying-W, and my wife wanted to call it the Suzy-Q. But one of our sons liked the Bar-J, and the other preferred the Lazy-Y. So we compromised and called it the Flying-W, Suzy-Q, Bar-J, Lazy-Y Ranch." Their friend asked, "Well, where are your cattle?" The man replied, "We don't have any. None of them survived the branding!"

The author is unknown who said, "An infant is born with a clenched fist; a man dies with an open hand. Life has a way of prying free the things we think are so important."

Gary Redding tells this story about Senator Paul Tsongas of Massachusetts. In January 1984, he announced that he would retire from the U.S. Senate and not seek reelection. Tsongas was a rising political star. He was a strong favorite to be reelected, and had even been mentioned as a potential future candidate for the presidency or vice presidency of the United States.

A few weeks before his announcement, Tsongas had learned he had a form of lymphatic cancer that could not be cured but could be treated. In all likelihood, it would not greatly affect his physical abilities or life expectancy. The illness did not force Tsongas out of the Senate, but it did force him to face the reality of his own mortality. He would not be able to do everything he might want to do. So what were the things he really wanted to do in the time he had?

He decided that what he wanted most out of his life, what he would not give up if he could not have everything, was being with his family and watching his children grow up. He would rather do that than shape the nation's laws or get his name in the history books.

Shortly after his decision was announced, a friend wrote a note to congratulate Tsongas on having his priorities straight. The note read: "Nobody on his death bed ever said, 'I wish I had spent more time on my business.'"

THREE

THE MOST IMPORTANT INGREDIENT
OF LEADERSHIP:
INTEGRITY

The dictionary defines *integrity* as "the state of being complete, unified." When I have integrity, my words and my deeds match up. I am who I am, no matter where I am or who I am with.

Sadly, integrity is a vanishing commodity today. Personal standards are crumbling in a world that has taken to hot pursuit of personal pleasure and shortcuts to success.

On a job application one question read, "Have you ever been arrested?" The applicant printed the word *No* in the space. The next question was a follow-up to the first. It asked, "Why?" Not realizing he did not have to answer this part, the "honest" and rather naïve applicant wrote, "I guess it's because I never got caught."

A Jeff Danziger cartoon shows a company president announcing to his staff, "Gentlemen, this year the trick is honesty." From one side of the conference table, a vice president gasps, "Brilliant." Across the table, another VP mutters, "But so risky."

In a cartoon in the *New Yorker*, two clean-shaven middle-aged men are sitting together in a jail cell. One inmate turns to the other and says, "All along, I thought our level of corruption fell well within community standards."

The White House, the Pentagon, Capitol Hill, the church, the sports arena, the academy, even the day care center have all been hit hard by scandal. In every case, the lack of credibility can be traced back to the level of integrity of the individuals within those organizations and institutions.

A person with integrity does not have divided loyalties (that's duplicity), nor is he or she merely pretending (that's hypocrisy). People with integrity are "whole" people; they can be identified by their single-mindedness. People with integrity have nothing to hide and nothing to fear. Their lives are open books. V. Gilbert Beers says, "A person of integrity is one who has established a system of values against which all of life is judged."

Integrity is not what we do so much as who we are. And who we are, in turn, determines what we do. Our system of values is so much a part of us we cannot separate it from ourselves. It becomes the navigating system that guides us. It establishes priorities in our lives and judges what we will accept or reject.

We are all faced with conflicting desires. No one, no matter how "spiritual," can avoid this battle. Integrity is the factor that determines which one will prevail. We struggle daily with situations that demand decisions between what we want to do and what we ought to do. Integrity establishes the ground rules for resolving these tensions. It determines who we are and how we will respond before the conflict even appears. Integrity welds what we say, think, and do into a whole person so that permission is never granted for one of those to be out of sync.

Integrity binds our person together and fosters a spirit of contentment within us. It will not allow our lips to violate our hearts. When integrity is the referee, we will be consistent; our beliefs will be mirrored by our conduct. There will be no discrepancy between what we appear to be and what our family knows we are, whether in times of prosperity or adversity. Integrity allows us to predetermine what we will be regardless of circumstances, persons involved, or the places of our testing.

Integrity is not only the referee between two desires. It is the pivotal point between a happy person and a divided spirit. It frees us to be whole persons no matter what comes our way.

"The first key to greatness," Socrates reminds us, "is to be in reality what we appear to be." Too often we try to be a "human doing" before we have become a "human being." To earn trust a leader has to be authentic. For that to happen, one must come across as a good musical composition does—the words and the music must match.

If what I say and what I do are the same, the results are consistent. For example:

I say to the employees: "Be at work on time."	I arrive at work on time.	They will be on time.
I say to the employees: "Be positive."	I exhibit a positive attitude.	They will be positive.
I say to the employees: "Put the customer first."	I put the customer first.	They will put the customer first.

If what I say and do are not the same, the results are inconsistent. For example:

I say to the employees: "Be at work on time."	I arrive at work late.	Some will be on time; some won't.
I say to the employees: "Be positive."	I exhibit a negative attitude.	Some will be positive; some won't.
I say to the employees: "Put the customer first."	I put myself first.	Some will put customers first; some won't.

Eighty-nine percent of what people learn comes through visual stimulation, 10 percent through audible stimulation, and 1 percent through other senses. So it makes sense that the more followers see and hear their leader being consistent in action and word, the greater their consistency and loyalty. *What they hear, they understand. What they see, they believe!*

> Integrity is not what we do as much as who we are.

Too often we attempt to motivate our followers with gimmicks that are short-lived and shallow. What people need is not a motto to say, but a model to see.

THE CREDIBILITY ACID TEST

The more credible you are, the more confidence people place in you, thereby allowing you the privilege of influencing their lives. The less credible you are, the less confidence people place in you and the more quickly you lose your position of influence.

> Image is what people think we are. Integrity is what we really are.

Many leaders who have attended my conferences have said to me, "I hope you can give me some insights into how I can change my company." My response is always the same: "My goal is to inspire you to change; if that happens, the organization will also be changed." As I have said time and time again, everything rises and falls on leadership. The secret to rising and not falling is integrity. Let's look at some reasons why integrity is so important.

1. INTEGRITY BUILDS TRUST

Dwight Eisenhower said:

> In order to be a leader a man must have followers. And to have followers, a man must have their confidence. Hence, the supreme quality for a leader is unquestionably integrity. Without it, no real

success is possible, no matter whether it is on a section gang, a football field, in an army, or in an office. If a man's associates find him guilty of being phony, if they find that he lacks forthright integrity, he will fail. His teachings and actions must square with each other. The first great need, therefore, is integrity and high purpose.[1]

Pieter Bruyn, a Dutch specialist in administration, holds that authority is not the power a boss has over subordinates, but rather the boss's ability to influence subordinates to recognize and accept that power. He calls it a "bargain": Subordinates tacitly agree to accept the boss as boss in return for being offered the kind of leadership *they* can accept. What does Bruyn's theory boil down to? Quite simply, the manager must build—and maintain—credibility. Subordinates must be able to trust that their boss will act in good faith toward them.

Too often people who are responsible for leading look to the organization to make people responsible to follow. They ask for a new title, another position, an organization chart, and a new policy to curtail insubordination. Sadly they never get enough authority to become effective. Why? They are looking to the outside when their problem is on the inside. They lack authority because they lack integrity.

Only 45 percent of four hundred managers in a Carnegie-Mellon survey believed their top management; a third distrusted their immediate bosses.[2] With so much depending on credibility and trust, someone in every organization must provide the leadership to improve these numbers.

Cavett Roberts said: "If my people understand me, I'll get their attention. If my people trust me, I'll get their action." For a leader to have the authority to lead, he needs more than the title on his door. He has to have the trust of those who are following him.

2. INTEGRITY HAS HIGH INFLUENCE VALUE

Emerson said, "Every great institution is the lengthened shadow of a single man. His character determines the character of the organization."

That statement "lines up" with the words of Will Rogers, who said, "People's minds are changed through observation and not argument." People do what people see.

According to 1,300 senior executives who responded to a recent survey, integrity is the human quality most necessary to business success. Seventy-one percent put it at the top of a list of sixteen traits responsible for enhancing an executive's effectiveness.

Regrettably we tend to forget the high influence value of integrity in the home. R. C. Sproul, in his book *Objections Answered*, tells about a young Jewish boy who grew up in Germany many years ago. The lad had a profound sense of admiration for his father, who saw to it that the life of the family revolved around the religious practices of their faith. The father led them to the synagogue faithfully.

In his teen years, however, the boy's family was forced to move to another town in Germany. This town had no synagogue, only a Lutheran church. The life of the community revolved around the Lutheran church; all the best people belonged to it. Suddenly, the father announced to the family that they were all going to abandon their Jewish traditions and join the Lutheran church. When the stunned family asked why, the father explained that it would be good for his business. The youngster was bewildered and confused. His deep disappointment soon gave way to anger and a kind of intense bitterness that plagued him throughout his life.

Later he left Germany and went to England to study. Each day found him at the British Museum, formulating his ideas and composing a book. In that book he introduced a whole new worldview and conceived a movement that was designed to change the world. He described religion as the "opiate for the masses." He committed the people who followed him to life without God. His ideas became the norm for the governments for almost half the world's people. His name? Karl Marx, founder of the Communist movement. The history of the twentieth century, and perhaps beyond, was significantly affected because one father let his values become distorted.

3. INTEGRITY FACILITATES HIGH STANDARDS

Leaders must live by higher standards than their followers. This insight is exactly opposite of most people's thoughts concerning leadership. In a world of perks and privileges that accompany the climb to success, little thought is given to the responsibilities of the upward journey. Leaders can give up anything except responsibility, either for themselves or their organizations. John D. Rockefeller Jr. said, "I believe that every right implies a responsibility; every opportunity, an obligation; every possession, a duty." The diagram below illustrates this principle.

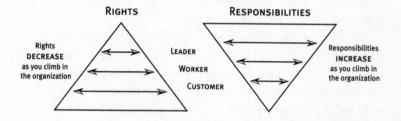

Too many people are ready to assert their rights, but not to assume their responsibilities. Richard L. Evans, in his book *An Open Road*, said:

> It is priceless to find a person who will take responsibility, who will finish and follow through to the final detail—to know when someone has accepted an assignment that it will be effectively, conscientiously completed. But when half-finished assignments keep coming back—to check on, to verify, to edit, to interrupt thought, and to take repeated attention—obviously someone has failed to follow the doctrine of completed work.

Tom Robbins said, "Don't let yourself be victimized by the age you live in. It's not the time that will bring us down, any more than it's society. There's a tendency today to absolve individuals of moral responsibility and treat them as victims of social circumstance. You buy that and you pay with your soul. What limits people is lack of character." When the character of leaders is low, so are their standards.

4. INTEGRITY RESULTS IN A SOLID REPUTATION, NOT JUST AN IMAGE

Image is what people think we are. Integrity is what we really are.

Two old ladies were walking around a somewhat overcrowded English country churchyard and came upon a tombstone. The inscription said: "Here lies John Smith, a politician and an honest man."

"Good heavens!" said one lady to the other. "Isn't it awful that they had to put two people in the same grave!"

All of us have known those who were not the same on the outside as they were inside. Sadly, many who have worked harder on their images than on their integrity don't understand when they suddenly "fall." Even friends who thought they knew them are surprised.

In ancient China the people wanted security against the barbaric hordes to the north, so they built the great wall. It was so high they believed no one could climb over it and so thick nothing could break it down. They settled back to enjoy their security. During the first hundred years of the wall's existence, China was invaded three times. Not once did the barbaric hordes break down the wall or climb over it. Each time they bribed a gatekeeper and then marched right through the gates. The Chinese were so busy relying on the walls of stone that they forgot to teach integrity to their children.

Your answers to the following questions will determine if you are into image-building instead of integrity-building:

Consistency:	Are you the same person no matter who you are with?
Choices:	Do you make decisions that are best for others when another choice would benefit you?
Credit:	Are you quick to recognize others for their efforts and contributions to your success?

Thomas Macauley said, "The measure of a man's real character is what he would do if he would never be found out." Life is like a vise; at times it will squeeze us. At those moments of pressure, whatever is inside will be found out. We cannot give what we do not have. Image promises much but produces little. Integrity never disappoints.

5. INTEGRITY MEANS LIVING IT MYSELF *BEFORE* LEADING OTHERS

We cannot lead anyone else farther than we have been ourselves. Too many times we are so concerned about the product that we try to shortcut the process. There are no shortcuts when integrity is involved. Eventually truth will always be exposed.

Recently I heard of a man who interviewed a consultant to some of the largest U.S. companies about their quality control. The consultant said, "In quality control, we are not concerned about the product. We are concerned about the process. If the process is right, the product is guaranteed." The same holds true for integrity; it guarantees credibility.

When the *Challenger* exploded, America was stunned to discover that Quality Control had warned NASA that the space shuttle was not fully prepared to go. But production said, "The show must go on!" *Crash*, just like many leaders.

HOLD IT! I CAN'T SWIM!

I remember hearing my basketball coach, Don Neff, repeatedly emphasize to our team, "You play like you practice; you play like you practice." When we fail to follow this principle, we fail to reach our personal potentials. When leaders fail to follow this principle, eventually they lose their credibility.

6. INTEGRITY HELPS A LEADER BE CREDIBLE, NOT JUST CLEVER

I once had dinner with Fred Smith. This wise businessman shared with me the difference between being clever and being credible. He said that clever leaders never last. That statement reminded me of the words of Peter Drucker, given to pastors gathered to discuss important issues in the church:

> The final requirement of effective leadership is to earn trust. Otherwise there won't be any followers . . . A leader is someone who has followers. To trust a leader, it is not necessary to agree with him. Trust is the conviction that the leader means what he says. It is a belief in something very old-fashioned called "integrity." A leader's actions and a leader's professed beliefs must be congruent or at least compatible. Effective leadership—and again this is very old wisdom—is not based on being clever; it is primarily on being consistent.[3]

Leaders who are sincere don't have to advertise the fact. It's visible in everything they do and soon becomes common knowledge to everyone. Likewise, insincerity cannot be hidden, disguised, or covered up, no matter how competent a manager may otherwise be.

The only way to keep the goodwill and high esteem of the people you work with is to deserve it. No one can fool all of the people all of the time. Each of us, eventually, is recognized for exactly what we are—not what we try to appear to be.

Ann Landers said, "People of integrity expect to be believed. They also know time will prove them right and are willing to wait."

7. INTEGRITY IS A HARD-WON ACHIEVEMENT

Integrity is not a given factor in everyone's life. It is a result of self-discipline, inner trust, and a decision to be relentlessly honest in all situations in our lives. Unfortunately in today's world, strength of character is a rare commodity. As a result, we have few contemporary models of integrity. Our culture has produced few enduring heroes, few models of virtue. We have become a nation of imitators, but there are few leaders worth imitating.

The meaning of integrity has been eroded. Drop the word into conversations in Hollywood, on Wall Street, even on Main Street, and you'll get blank stares in return. For most Americans, the word conjures up ideas of prudishness or narrow-mindedness. In an age when the meanings of words are manipulated, foundational values such as integrity can be pulverized overnight.

Integrity is antithetical to the spirit of our age. The overarching philosophy of life that guides our culture revolves around a materialistic, consumer mentality. The craving need of the moment supersedes consideration of values that have eternal significance.

When we sell out to someone else, we also sell out ourselves. Hester H. Chomondelay underscores this truth in his short poem, "Judas":

> Still as of old
> Men by themselves are priced—
> For thirty pieces Judas sold
> Himself, not Christ.

Billy Graham said, "Integrity is the glue that holds our way of life together. We must constantly strive to keep our integrity intact.

"When wealth is lost, nothing is lost; when health is lost, something is lost; when character is lost, all is lost."[4]

To build your life on the foundation of integrity, use the following poem ("Am I True to Myself?" by Edgar Guest) as a "Mirror Test" to evaluate how you're doing.

I have to live with myself, and so
I want to be fit for myself to know,
I want to be able, as days go by,
Always to look myself straight in the eye;
I don't want to stand, with the setting sun,
And hate myself for things I have done.
I don't want to keep on a closet shelf
A lot of secrets about myself,
And fool myself, as I come and go,
Into thinking that nobody else will know
The kind of man I really am;
I don't want to dress up myself in sham.
I want to go out with my head erect,
I want to deserve all men's respect;
But here in the struggle for fame and pelf
I want to be able to like myself.
I don't want to look at myself and know
That I'm bluster and bluff and empty show.
I can never hide myself from me;
I see what others may never see;
I know what others may never know,
I never can fool myself, and so,
Whatever happens, I want to be
Self-respecting and conscience free.

Next, take the "Mentor Test." It asks, "Am I true to my leader?" Joseph Bailey interviewed more than thirty top executives. He found that all learned firsthand from a mentor.[5] Ralph Waldo Emerson said, "Our chief want in life is somebody who shall make us what we can be." When we find that person, we need to check our growth on a regular basis, asking, "Am I totally availing myself of the teaching I am receiving?" Taking shortcuts in this process will hurt both your mentor and you.

Finally, take the "Masses Test." It asks, "Am I true to my followers?" As leaders, we quickly understand that wrong decisions not only adversely affect us, but they affect those who follow us. However, making a bad decision because of wrong motives is totally different. Before reaching for the reins of leadership, we must realize that we teach what we know and reproduce what we are. Integrity is an inside job.

Advocates of modeling dependability before followers, James M. Kouzes and Barry Z. Posner report in their book, *The Leadership Challenge*, that followers expect four things from their leaders: honesty, competence, vision, and inspiration.[6]

Write out what you value in life. A conviction is a belief or principle that you regularly model, one for which you would be willing to die. What are your convictions?

Ask someone who knows you well what areas of your life he sees as consistent (you do what you say) and what areas he sees as inconsistent (you say but don't always live).

YOU WILL ONLY BECOME WHAT YOU ARE BECOMING RIGHT NOW

Though you cannot go back
and make a brand-new start, my friend.
Anyone can start from now
and make a brand-new end.

FOUR

THE ULTIMATE TEST OF LEADERSHIP:
CREATING POSITIVE CHANGE

Change the leader, change the organization. Everything rises and falls on leadership! However, I have found that it's not easy to change leaders. In fact, I've discovered that leaders resist change as much as followers do. The result? Unchanged leaders equals unchanged organizations. People do what people see.

PROFILE OF A LEADER IN TROUBLE

Notice that of the twelve trouble spots for a leader listed below, five deal with an unwillingness to change. That spells trouble for the organization.

- Has a poor understanding of people
- Lacks imagination
- Has personal problems
- Passes the buck
- Feels secure and satisfied
- Is not organized
- Flies into rages

- Will not take a risk
- Is insecure and defensive
- Stays inflexible
- Has no team spirit
- Fights change

Niccolò Machiavelli said, "There is nothing more difficult to take in hand, more perilous to conduct or more uncertain in its success, than to take the lead in the introduction of a new order of things."

The first order of things to be changed is me, the leader. After I consider how hard it is to change myself, then I will understand the challenge of trying to change others. This is the ultimate test of leadership.

A Middle-Eastern mystic said:

> I was a revolutionary when I was young and all my prayer to God was: "Lord, give me the energy to change the world." As I approached middle age and realized that my life was half gone without my changing a single soul, I changed my prayer to: "Lord, give me the grace to change all those who come into contact with me, just my family and friends, and I shall be satisfied." Now that I am an old man and my days are numbered, I have begun to see how foolish I have been. My one prayer now is: "Lord, give me the grace to change myself." If I had prayed for this right from the start, I would not have wasted my life.[1]

Howard Hendricks, in his book *Teaching to Change Lives*, throws a challenge out to every potential leader:

> Write down somewhere in the margins on this page your answer to this question: How have you changed . . . lately? In the last week, let's say? Or in the last month? The last year? Can you be very specific? Or must your answer be incredibly vague? You say you're

growing. Okay . . . how? "Well," you say, "In all kinds of ways." Great! Name one. You see, effective teaching comes only through a changed person. The more you change, the more you become an instrument of change in the lives of others. If you want to become a change agent, you also must change.[2]

Hendricks could have also said, "If you want to continue leading, you must continue changing." Many leaders are no longer leading. They have become like Henry Ford, who is described in Robert Lacy's best-selling biography, *Ford: The Man and the Machine*.[3] Lacy says Ford was a man who loved his Model T so much that he didn't want to change a bolt on it. He even kicked out William Knudsen, his ace production man, because Knudsen thought he saw the sun setting on the Model T. That occurred in 1912, when the Model T was only four years old and at the crest of its popularity. Ford had just returned from a European jaunt, and he went to a Highland Park, Michigan, garage and saw the new design created by Knudsen.

> Change the leader—change the organization.

On-the-scene mechanics recorded how Ford momentarily went berserk. He spied the gleaming red lacquer sheen on a new, low-slung version of the Model T that he considered a monstrous perversion of his beloved Model T design. "Ford had his hands in his pockets, and he walked around that car three or four times," recounted an eyewitness. "It was a four-door job, and the top was down. Finally, he got to the left-hand side of the car, and he takes his hands out, gets hold of the door, and bang! He ripped the door right off! . . . How the man done it, I don't know! He jumped in there, and bang goes the other door. Bang goes the windshield. He jumps over the back seat and starts pounding on the top. He rips the top with the heel of his shoe. He wrecked the car as much as he could."

Knudsen left for General Motors. Henry Ford nursed along the Model T, but design changes in competitors' models made it more old-fashioned than he would admit. Competitive necessity finally backed him into making the Model A, though his heart was never in it. Even though General Motors was nipping at Ford's heels, the inventor wanted life to freeze where it was.

Underpinning this theme, William A. Hewitt, Chairman of Deere and Company, says, "To be a leader you must preserve all through your life the attitude of being receptive to new ideas. The quality of leadership you will give will depend upon your ability to evaluate new ideas, to separate change for the sake of change from change for the sake of me."

THE LEADER AS A CHANGE AGENT

Once the leader has personally changed and discerned the difference between novel change and needed change, then that leader must become a change agent. In this world of discontinuities and rapid change, the leader must be out in front to encourage change and growth and to show the way to bring it about. He must first understand the two important requisites to bringing about change: knowing the technical requirements of the change, and understanding the attitude and motivational demands for bringing it about.

> When you're through changing, you're through.

Both requisites are critically necessary. More often than not, though, when results fail to change, it is because of inadequate or inappropriate motivation, not a lack of technical smarts.

A manager usually will be more skilled in the technical requirements of change, whereas the leader will have a better understanding of the attitudinal and motivational demands that the followers need. Note the difference: In the beginning the skills of a leader are essential. No change will ever occur if the psychological needs are unmet. Once change has begun, the skills of a manager are needed to maintain needed change.

Bobb Biehl, in his book *Increasing Your Leadership Confidence*, states it this way: "A change can make sense logically, but still lead to anxiety in the psychological dimension. Everyone needs a niche, and when the niche starts to change after we've become comfortable in it, it causes stress and insecurities. So before introducing change, we have to consider the psychological dimension."[4]

A good exercise when you face change is to make a list of the logical advantages and disadvantages that should result from the change, and then make another list indicating the psychological impact. Just seeing this on a sheet of paper can be clarifying. You may find yourself saying, "I don't like to admit it, but I'm insecure at this point, even though the change makes sense logically."

Another possibility is that a change you're considering may not affect your psychological security, but it doesn't make sense logically when you examine the advantages and disadvantages. The key is to distinguish between the logical and the psychological aspects of any change.

A HISTORICAL ACCOUNT OF RESISTANCE TO CHANGE

There is nothing more difficult to undertake, more perilous to conduct, or more uncertain in its success than introducing change. Why? The leader has for enemies all those who have done well under the old conditions and only lukewarm defenders in those who may do well with the change.

Resistance to change is universal. It invades all classes and cultures. It seizes every generation by the throat and attempts to stop all forward movement toward progress. Many well-educated people, after being confronted with truth, have been unwilling to change their minds.

> Growth equals change.

For example, for centuries people believed that Aristotle was right when he said that the heavier an object, the faster it would fall to earth. Aristotle was regarded as the greatest thinker of all time, and surely he could not be wrong. All it would have taken was for one brave person to take two objects, one heavy and one light, and drop them from a great height to see whether or not the heavier object landed first. But no one stepped forward until nearly two thousand years after Aristotle's death. In 1589, Galileo summoned learned professors to the base of the Leaning Tower of Pisa. Then he went to the top and pushed off two weights, one weighing ten pounds and the other weighing one pound. Both landed at the same time. But the power of belief in the conventional wisdom was so strong that the professors denied what they had seen. They continued to say Aristotle was right.

With his telescope, Galileo proved the theory of Copernicus, that the earth is not the center of the universe; the earth and the planets revolve around the sun. Yet when he tried to change people's beliefs, he was thrown into prison and spent the rest of his life under house arrest.

Resisting change can unwittingly affect one's health and life, as the following account portrays. Hippocrates described scurvy in ancient times. The disease seemed to especially plague armies in the field and cities that were under siege for long periods of time. Later, following the discovery of America, when long sea voyages became common, scurvy became rampant among sailors. Little was known about what caused scurvy and less about its cure, although elaborate theories and remedies were prescribed. None of them was completely effective, and most were worthless.

In 1553, Cartier made his second voyage to Newfoundland. Of his 103-man crew, 100 developed agonizing scurvy and were in great anguish when the Iroquois Indians of Quebec came to their rescue with what was described as a "miraculous cure." The Iroquois Indians gave the sick sailors an infusion of bark and leaves of the pine tree.

In 1553, Admiral Sir Richard Hawkins noted that during his career on the high seas, ten thousand seamen under his command had died of scurvy. He also recorded that in his experience sour oranges and lemons had been most effective in curing the disease. Yet these observations had no sweeping effect in bringing about an awareness of what could prevent scurvy, and the observations of this admiral went unheeded.

James Lind, a British naval surgeon, who later became the chief physician of the Naval Hospital at Portsmouth, England, published a book in 1753 in which he stated explicitly that scurvy could be eliminated simply by supplying sailors with lemon juice. He cited many case histories from his experience as a naval surgeon at sea; he proved that such things as mustard cress, tamarinds, oranges, and lemons would prevent scurvy. In fact, anything that contains enough vitamin C, which is most abundant in citrus fruit, tomatoes, and to a lesser degree in most green vegetables and other fruits, will prevent scurvy.

You might rightfully expect that Dr. Lind would have been highly honored and praised for this great contribution, but the reverse is true. He was ridiculed. He became frustrated and remarked bitterly, "Some persons cannot be brought to believe that a disease so fatal and so dreaded can be cured or prevented by such easy means." They would have more faith in an elaborate composition dignified with the title of "an antiscorbutic golden elixir" or the like. The "some persons" to whom Dr. Lind referred were My Lords of the Admiralty and other physicians. In fact, they ignored Dr. Lind's advice for forty years. One sea captain did take his advice—the now-famous Captain James Cook, who stocked his ships with an ample supply of fresh fruits.

The Royal Society honored Captain Cook in 1776 for his success, but the officials of the navy ignored his report. Not until 1794, the year of Dr. Lind's death, was a British navy squadron supplied with lemon juice before a voyage. On that voyage, which lasted twenty-three weeks, there was not one case of scurvy, yet another decade passed before regulations were enacted requiring sailors to drink a daily ration of lemon juice to prevent scurvy. With this enactment, scurvy disappeared from the British Navy.[5]

The needless loss of life simply because masses of people were resistant to change was more than unfortunate. It was outrageous. Don't let your attitude toward change or your own predisposition to avoid it create detrimental hindrances to your own personal success as a leader.

How Do You Write the Word "Attitude"?

Directions:
1. Write the word *attitude* on the left line with your "writing" hand.
2. Write the word *attitude* on the right line with your other hand.

The word *attitude* written with your writing hand.

The word *attitude* written with your other hand.

Application:

When you look at the word *attitude* written by the hand you do not write with, you see a picture of the kind of attitude we usually have when we are trying to do something new. As one person said, "Nothing should ever be done for the first time."

WHY PEOPLE RESIST CHANGE

In a *Peanuts* cartoon, Charlie Brown says to Linus: "Perhaps you can give me an answer, Linus. What would you do if you felt that no one liked you?" Linus replies, "I'd try to look at myself objectively, and see what I could do to *improve*. That's *my* answer, Charlie Brown." To which Charlie replies, "I *hate* that answer!"

There are a number of reasons why many of us, like Charlie Brown, resist change.

THE CHANGE ISN'T SELF-INITIATED

When people lack ownership of an idea, they usually resist it, even when it is in their best interest! They simply don't like the idea of being manipulated or feeling like pawns of the system. Wise leaders allow followers to give input and be a part of the process of change. Most of the time the key to my attitude about change is whether I am initiating it (in which case I am all for it) or someone else is imposing the change on me (which tends to make me more resistant).

ROUTINE IS DISRUPTED

Habits allow us to do things without much thought, which is why most of us have so many of them. Habits are not instincts. They are acquired reactions. They don't just happen; they are caused. First we form habits, but then our habits form us. Change threatens our habit patterns and forces us to think, reevaluate, and sometimes unlearn past behavior.

When I was a teenager, I became interested in golf. Regrettably, I taught myself instead of taking lessons. After a few years and the innocent acquisition of many bad habits, I played a game of golf with an excellent player. At the close of the round, he jokingly said my main problem seemed to be that I was too close to the ball after I hit it! Then he seriously offered to help me. He shared honestly how I would need to make some changes if my golf game was to improve. When I asked him to specify what changes I needed to make, he said, "Everything!" For the next year I had to unlearn old habits. It was one of the most difficult experiences of my life. Many times I was tempted to return to my old habits for temporary relief from working so hard and still playing so badly.

CHANGE CREATES FEAR OF THE UNKNOWN

Change means traveling in uncharted waters, and this causes our insecurities to rise. Therefore, many people are more comfortable with old problems than with new solutions. They are like the congregation that desperately needed a new building but were afraid to venture out. During a service some plaster fell from the ceiling and hit the chairman of the board. Immediately a meeting was called and the following decisions were made:

One:	We will build a new church.
Two:	We will build a new church on the same site as the old one.
Three:	We will use the materials of the old church to build the new one.
Four	We will worship in the old church until the new church is built.

Some people are open to change as long as it doesn't inconvenience them or cost anything.

The Purpose of the Change Is Unclear

Employees resist change when they hear about it from a secondhand source. When a decision has been made, the longer it takes for employees to hear and the further the desired change is from the decision maker, the more resistance it will receive. That's why decisions should be made at the lowest level possible. The decision maker, because of close proximity to the issue, will make a better decision, and those most affected by the decision will know it quickly by hearing it from a source close to them and to the problem.

Change Creates Fear of Failure

Elbert Hubbard said that the greatest mistake a person can make is to be afraid of making one. It is tragic when success has "gone to my head." It is even more tragic if failure goes to my head. When this happens, I begin to agree with Larry Anderson, the pitcher for the San Diego Padres. He said, "If at first you don't succeed, failure may be your thing." Too many people, fearing that failure is their thing, hold tenaciously to whatever they feel comfortable with and continually resist change.

The Rewards for Change Don't Match the Effort Change Requires

People will not change until they perceive that the advantages of changing outweigh the disadvantages of continuing with the way things are. What leaders sometimes fail to recognize is that the followers will always weigh the advantage/disadvantage issue in light of personal gain/loss, not organizational gain/loss.

People Are Too Satisfied with the Way Things Are

As the following story from *Parables* reveals, many organizations and people will choose to die before they will choose to change.

In the 1940s, the Swiss watch was the most prestigious and best quality watch in the world. Consequently, 80 percent of the watches sold in the world were made in Switzerland. In the late '50s, the digital watch was presented to the leaders of the Swiss watch company. They rejected this new idea because they knew they already had the best watch and the best watchmakers. The man who developed the digital watch subsequently sold the idea to Seiko.

In 1940, Swiss watch-making companies employed eighty thousand people. Today they employ eighteen thousand. In 1940, 80 percent of the watches sold in the world were made in Switzerland. Today 80 percent of the watches are digital. This story represents what happens to many organizations and people: We choose to die rather than choose to change.

CHANGE WON'T HAPPEN WHEN PEOPLE ENGAGE IN NEGATIVE THINKING

Regardless of his state in the present, the negative thinker finds disappointment in the future. The epitaph on a negative person's headstone should read, "I expected this." This type of thinking can best be described by a sign I read several years ago in an office building:

Don't look—you might see.
Don't listen—you might hear.
Don't think—you might learn.
Don't make a decision—you might be wrong.
Don't walk—you might stumble.
Don't run—you might fall.
Don't live—you might die.

I would like to add one more thought to this depressing list:

Don't change—you might grow.

THE FOLLOWERS LACK RESPECT FOR THE LEADER

When followers don't like the leader who oversees the change, their feelings won't allow them to look at the change objectively. In other words, people view the change according to the way they view the change agent.

One of the principles I share in leadership conferences is, "You've got to love 'em before you can lead 'em." When you love your followers genuinely and correctly, they'll respect and follow you through many changes.

THE LEADER IS SUSCEPTIBLE TO FEELINGS OF PERSONAL CRITICISM

Sometimes leaders resist change. For example, if a leader has developed a program that is now being phased out for something better, he or she may feel the change is a personal attack and will react defensively.

For growth and continual effectiveness, every organization must go through a continuous four-stage cycle of create, conserve, criticize, and change. The figure below illustrates the cycle.

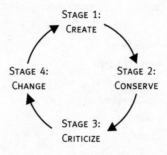

Stages 1 and 4 are the offensive functions of an organization. Stages 2 and 3 are the defensive functions. Either the creators handle criticism positively and begin to make changes, or they will be replaced by those who will embrace change and, therefore, create.

CHANGE MAY MEAN PERSONAL LOSS

Whenever change is imminent, the question on everyone's mind is, "How will this affect me?" Usually there are three groups of people within the organization: (1) those who will lose; (2) those who are neutral; and (3) those who will benefit. Each group is different and must be handled with sensitivity, but also with straightforwardness.

CHANGE REQUIRES ADDITIONAL COMMITMENT

Time is the most precious commodity for many people. Whenever change is about to happen, we all look to see how it will affect our time. Usually we conclude that increased change will be fine *if* it does not increase our time commitment. Sidney Howard said that half of knowing what you want is knowing what you must give up before you get it. When the cost of change is time, many will resist the change.

When it comes to the commitment of time, the leader must determine if the person is *unwilling* or *unable* to change. Willingness deals with attitude, and there is little you can do if your followers resist change because of attitude. But ability to change deals with perspective. Many people are willing to change but, because of the way they perceive their present circumstances and responsibilities, they are unable to change. At this point, the leader can help by prioritizing tasks, eliminating nonessentials, and focusing on the consequential value of changing.

NARROW-MINDEDNESS THWARTS ACCEPTANCE OF NEW IDEAS

In 1993, approximately sixteen hundred people belonged to the International Flat Earth Research Society of America. Their president, Charles K. Johnson, said he's been a flat-earther all his life. "When I saw the globe in grade school I didn't accept it then and I don't accept it now."

That reminds me of the man who lived in Maine and turned one hundred years of age. A reporter drove up from New York City to interview the old man. Sitting on the front porch, the reporter said, "I'll bet you've seen a lot of changes in your lifetime." The old man replied, "Yes, and I've been agin' every one of them."

Tradition Resists Change

I love this joke: "How many people does it take to change a lightbulb?" Answer: "Four. One to change the bulb and three to reminisce about how good the old lightbulb was."

People like that remind me of the old army sergeant who was put in charge of a plot of grass in front of administrative headquarters in a camp in Michigan. The sergeant promptly delegated the job to a buck private and told him to water the grass every day at five o'clock. The private did this conscientiously. One day there was a terrific thunderstorm, and the sergeant walked into the barracks and saw the private doing bunk fatigue.

"What's the matter with you?" the sergeant bellowed. "It's five o'clock, and you're supposed to be out watering the grass!"

"But, Sergeant," the private said, looking confused, "it's raining; look at the thunderstorm."

"So what?" yelled the sergeant. "You've got a raincoat, haven't you?"

Cornfield's Law says that nothing is ever done until everyone is convinced that it ought to be done, and has been convinced for so long that it is now time to do something else.

A CHECKLIST FOR CHANGE

Below are the questions you should review *before* attempting changes within an organization. When the questions can be answered with a yes, change tends to be easier. Questions that can only be answered with no (or maybe) usually indicate that change will be difficult.

YES   NO

____   ____   Will this change benefit the followers?

____   ____   Is this change compatible with the purpose of the organization?

____   ____   Is this change specific and clear?

____   ____   Are the top 20 percent (the influencers) in favor of this change?

____   ____   Is it possible to test this change before making a total commitment to it?

____   ____   Are physical, financial, and human resources available to make this change?

____   ____   Is this change reversible?

____   ____   Is this change the next obvious step?

____   ____   Does this change have both short- and long-range benefits?

____   ____   Is the leadership capable of bringing about this change?

____   ____   Is the timing right?

At times every leader feels like Lucy, when she was leaning against a fence with Charlie Brown. "I would like to change the world," she said. Charlie Brown asked, "Where would you start?" She replied, "I would start with you!"

The last question, "Is the timing right?" is the ultimate consideration for implementing change. A leader's success in bringing about change in others will happen only if the timing is right. In my book *The Winning Attitude*, this subject is discussed in short order:

> The wrong decision at the wrong time = disaster.
> The wrong decision at the right time = mistake.
> The right decision at the wrong time = unacceptance.
> The right decision at the right time = success.

People change when they *hurt* enough that they *have* to change;

learn enough that they *want* to change; *receive* enough that they are *able* to change. The leader must recognize when people are in one of these three stages. In fact, top leaders create an atmosphere that causes one of these three things to occur.[6]

THE EVOLUTIONARY PROCESS OF CHANGE

It is helpful to remember that change can be seen as either *revolutionary* (something totally different from what has been) or *evolutionary* (a refinement of what has been). It is usually easier to present change as a simple refinement of "the way we've been doing it" rather than something big, new, and completely different. When a proposal for change is introduced in the organization, people fall into five categories in terms of their response.

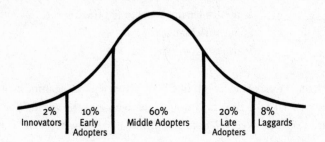

| 2%
Innovators | 10%
Early
Adopters | 60%
Middle Adopters | 20%
Late
Adopters | 8%
Laggards |

INNOVATORS ARE THE DREAMERS

They are the originators of new ideas and generally are not acknowledged as leaders or policy makers.

EARLY ADOPTERS ARE THOSE WHO KNOW A GOOD IDEA WHEN THEY SEE IT

Their opinions are respected in the organization. Although they did not create the idea, they will try to convince others to accept it.

MIDDLE ADOPTERS ARE THE MAJORITY

They will respond to the opinions of others. Generally they are reasonable in their analysis of a new idea, but inclined to maintain the status quo. They can be influenced by the positive or negative influencers of the organization.

LATE ADOPTERS ARE THE LAST GROUP TO ENDORSE AN IDEA

They often speak against proposed changes and may never verbally acknowledge acceptance. Generally they will adopt it if the majority demonstrates support.

LAGGARDS ARE ALWAYS AGAINST CHANGE

Their commitment is to the status quo and the past. Often they try to create division within the organization.[7]

The evolutionary process of successful change within an organization can be summed up in the eight steps that must occur as the organization moves from ignorance about the desired change and the effects it will have to a mind-set of willingness and innovation.

Step 1: **Ignorance.** No unified direction or sense of priorities is felt among the followers. They are "in the dark."

Step 2: **Information.** General information is given to the people. Initially the ideas for change are not embraced.

Step 3: **Infusion.** The penetration of new ideas into the status quo may cause confrontations with apathy, prejudice, and tradition. The general tendency is to focus on problems.

Step 4: **Individual Change.** The "early adopters" begin to see the benefits of the proposed change and embrace them. Personal convictions replace complacency.

Step 5: **Organizational Change.** Two sides of the issue are being discussed. Less defensiveness and more openness concerning proposed changes can be observed. The momentum shifts from antichange to prochange.

Step 6: **Awkward Application.** Some failures and some successes are experienced as the change is implemented. The learning process is rapid.

Step 7: **Integration.** Awkwardness begins to decrease, and the acceptance level increases. A growing sense of accomplishment and a secondary wave of results and successes occur.

Step 8: **Innovation.** Significant results create confidence and a willingness to take risks. The result is a willingness to change more rapidly and boldly.

As Step 8 is taken, the organization as a whole is more willing to go through the process again. The major effect of the process develops as the majority of the organization is exposed repeatedly to the new idea.

1st Exposure: "I reject that thought because it conflicts with my preconceived ideas."

2nd Exposure: "Well, I understand it, but I can't accept it."

3rd Exposure: "I agree with the idea but have reservations as to its use."

4th Exposure: "You know, that idea pretty well expresses the way I feel about the subject."

5th Exposure: "I used that idea today. It's terrific!"

6th Exposure: "I gave that idea to someone yesterday. In the truest sense of the word, that idea now belongs to me."

CREATING A CLIMATE FOR CHANGE

Human behavior studies show that people do not basically resist change; they resist "being changed."[8] This section will emphasize how to create an atmosphere that will encourage others to be changed. Unless people are changed, change will not happen. The first statement of this chapter read, "Change the leader, change the organization." Now we will start with the leader and develop a strategy for the organization.

The Leader Must Develop Trust with People

It is wonderful when the people believe in the leader. It is more wonderful when the leader believes in the people. When both are a reality, trust is the result. The more people trust the leader, the more willing they will be to accept the leader's proposed changes. Warren Bennis and Bert Nanus say that "trust is the emotional glue that binds followers and leaders together."[9] Abraham Lincoln said, "If you would win a man to your cause, first convince him that you are his true friend. Next, probe to discover what he wants to accomplish."

My first question to a leader who wants to make changes within an organization is always, "What is your relationship with your people?" If the relationship is positive, then the leader is ready to take the next step.

The Leader Must Make Personal Changes Before Asking Others to Change

Sadly, too many leaders are like my friend who made a list of New Year's resolutions: be nicer to people; eat nutritious food; be more giving to friends; cut down on sweets and fats; be less critical of others.

My friend showed me the list, and I was quite impressed. They were great goals. "But," I asked her, "do you think you'll be able to meet all of them?"

"Why should I?" she answered. "This list is for you!"

Andrew Carnegie said, "As I grow older, I pay less attention to what men say. I just watch what they do." Great leaders not only say what should be done, they show it!

GOOD LEADERS UNDERSTAND THE HISTORY OF THE ORGANIZATION

The longer an organization has gone without change, the more effort introducing it will require. Also, when change is implemented and the result is negative, people within the organization will be leery of embracing future changes. The opposite is also true. Successful changes in the past prepare people to readily accept more changes.

G. K. Chesterton suggests, "Don't take the fence down until you know the reason it was put up." It is important to know what happened in the past before making changes for the future.

PLACE INFLUENCERS IN LEADERSHIP POSITIONS

Leaders have two characteristics. First, they are going somewhere; and second, they are able to persuade other people to go with them. They are like the chairman of a large corporation, who was late for a meeting. Bolting into the room, he took the nearest available seat rather than moving to his accustomed spot. One of his young aides protested, "Please, sir, you should be at the head of the table." The executive, who had a healthy understanding of his place in the company, answered, "Son, wherever I sit is the head of the table."

CHECK THE "CHANGE IN YOUR POCKET"

Every leader is given a certain amount of "change" (emotional support in the form of bargaining chips) at the beginning of a relationship. If the relationship weakens, the leader gives up "change" until it is possible for him to become bankrupt with the organization. If the relationship strengthens, the leader receives "change" until it is possible for him to become rich with the organization. Always remember: *It takes "change" to make change*. The more "change" in the pocket of the leader, the more changes that can be made in the lives of the people. Sadly, the opposite is also true.

GOOD LEADERS SOLICIT THE SUPPORT OF INFLUENCERS *BEFORE* THE CHANGE IS MADE PUBLIC

This ten-item checklist includes all the steps a good leader will go through in soliciting support for a change from the major influencers in his organization.

1. List the major influencer(s) of the major groups within your organization.

2. How many will be affected *directly* by this change? (These people are the most important group.)

3. How many will be affected *indirectly* by this change?

4. How many will probably be positive?

5. How many will probably be negative?

6. Which group is the majority?

7. Which group is the most influential?

8. If the positive group is stronger, bring the influencers together for discussion.

9. If the negative group is stronger, meet with the influencers individually.

10. Know the "key" to each influencer.

DEVELOP A MEETING AGENDA THAT WILL ASSIST CHANGE

Every new idea goes through three phases: It will not work; it will cost too much; and, I thought it was a good idea all along.

A wise leader, understanding that people change through a process, will develop a meeting agenda to enhance this process. One that I have used for fifteen years has proved quite effective.

Information Items: Items of interest to those attending the meeting; positive items that boost morale. (This starts the meeting off on a high level.)

Study Items: Issues to be discussed but not voted on. (This allows the sharing of ideas without the pressure to represent a particular point of view.)

Action Items: Issues to be voted on that have previously been study items. (This allows discussion to be made that has already been processed. If major change is required, keep the issue in the study category until it has been allowed time for acceptance.)

ENCOURAGE THE INFLUENCERS TO INFLUENCE OTHERS INFORMALLY

Major changes should not surprise people. A "leadership leak" done properly will prepare the people for the formal meeting.

Each year I explain to my key leaders that they carry two buckets around with them. One bucket is filled with gasoline and the other with water. Whenever there is a "little fire" of contention within the organization because the people fear a possible change, the influencers are the first to hear about it. When they arrive on the scene, they will either throw the bucket of gasoline on the situation and really cause a problem, or they will throw the bucket of water on the little fire and extinguish the problem. In other words, key influences are either the leader's greatest asset or his greatest liability.

Leadership leaks should be planned and positive, preparing the people for the meeting where the change will be formally presented.

SHOW THE PEOPLE HOW THE CHANGE WILL BENEFIT THEM

Assumption: The proposed change is what is best for the people, not the leader. The people must be first.

A sign on the door in a bus station read: "For the convenience of others, please close the door." Too often the door remained open until the sign was changed to read: "For your *own* personal comfort, please close the door." The door was always shut. Too often leaders of an organization tend to think and lead from the company's perspective, not the people's.

GIVE THE PEOPLE OWNERSHIP OF THE CHANGE

Openness by the leader paves the way for ownership by the people. Without ownership, changes will be short-term. Changing people's habits and ways of thinking is like writing instructions in the snow during a snowstorm. Every twenty minutes the instructions must be rewritten, unless ownership is given along with the instructions.

HOW TO OFFER OWNERSHIP OF CHANGE TO OTHERS

1. Inform people in advance so they'll have time to think about the implications of the change and how it will affect them.

2. Explain the overall objectives of the change—the reasons for it and how and when it will occur.

3. Show people how the change will benefit them. Be honest with the employees who may lose out as a result of the change. Alert them early and provide assistance to help them find another job if necessary.

4. Ask those who will be affected by the change to participate in all stages of the change process.

5. Keep communication channels open. Provide opportunities for employees to discuss the change. Encourage questions, comments, and other feedback.

6. Be flexible and adaptable throughout the change process. Admit mistakes and make changes where appropriate.

7. Constantly demonstrate your belief in and commitment to the change. Indicate your confidence in their ability to implement the change.

8. Provide enthusiasm, assistance, appreciation, and recognition to those implementing the change.[10]

CHANGE WILL HAPPEN

The question should not be "Will we ever change?" but "When and how much will we change?" Nothing stays the same except the fact that change is always present. Even in the beginning, Adam reportedly said to Eve, as they were led out of paradise, "My dear, we live in a time of transition."

Charles Exley, CEO of NCR Corporation, said, "I've been in business thirty-six years. I've learned a lot and most of it doesn't apply anymore."

Writer Lincoln Barnett once described the excitement he shared with a group of students emerging from a physics lecture at the Institute for Advanced Study at Princeton. "How did it go?" someone asked.

"Wonderful!" Mr. Barnett replied. "Everything we knew last week isn't true."

Keeping current with the changes and relating them to the organization is a constant challenge for the leader. Leaders should be aware, for example, of information such as the following, which was outlined in an article written by Dr. Richard Caldwell.[11] He contrasts some of the values of the 1950s and those of the 1990s.

1950s	1990s
Saving	Spending
Delayed gratification	Instant gratification
Ozzie and Harriet	Latchkey kids
Certainty	Ambivalence
Orthodoxy	Skepticism
Investing	Leveraging

Neighborhood	Lifestyle
Middle class	Under class
Export	Import
Public virtue	Personal well-being
Mom and Dad	Nanny and day care
Press conference	Photo opportunity
Achievement	Fame
Knowledge	Credentials
Manufacturing	Service
Duty	Divorce
"We"	"Me"

NOT ALL CHANGE IS IMPROVEMENT, BUT WITHOUT CHANGE THERE CAN BE NO IMPROVEMENT

Change = Growth

or

Change = Grief

Change represents both possible opportunity and potential loss. My observation is that change becomes grief when:

- the change proposed is a bad idea.

- the change proposed is not accepted by the influencers.

- the change proposed is not presented effectively.

- the change proposed is self-serving to the leaders.

- the change proposed is based solely on the past.

- the changes proposed are too many, happening too quickly.

In 1950, *Fortune* magazine asked eleven distinguished Americans to predict what life would be like in 1980. In those days, the United States enjoyed a trade surplus of $3 billion, so no one predicted a trade deficit thirty years later. David Sarnoff, chairman of RCA, was sure that by

1980, ships, airplanes, locomotives, and even individual automobiles would be atomically fueled. He said that homes would have atomic generators and that guided missiles would transport mail and other freight over great distances. Henry R. Luce, editor-in-chief of *Time* magazine, predicted the end of poverty by 1980. Mathematician John von Neumann expected energy to be free thirty years later.

IT'S NEVER TOO LATE TO CHANGE

Max Depree said, "In the end, it is important to remember that we cannot become what we need to be by remaining what we are."[12] It's a fact that when you're through changing, you're through.

When you hear the name Alfred Nobel, what do you think of? The Nobel Peace Prize might come to mind. However, that's only chapter 2 of his story. Alfred Nobel was the Swedish chemist who made his fortune by inventing dynamite and the other powerful explosives used for weapons. When his brother died, one newspaper accidentally printed Alfred's obituary instead. It described the dead man as one who became rich by enabling people to kill each other in unprecedented numbers. Shaken by this assessment, Nobel resolved to use his fortune from then on to award accomplishments that benefited humanity. Nobel had the rare opportunity to evaluate his life at its end and yet live long enough to change that assessment.[13]

Comedian Jerry Lewis says that the best wedding gift he received was a film of the entire wedding ceremony. He says that when things got really bad in his marriage, he would go into a room, close the door, run the film backward, and walk out a free man.

I doubt you will be able to run the film backward or read your obituary in the newspaper. You can, however, make a choice today to change. And when change is successful, you will look back at it and call it growth.

FIVE

THE QUICKEST WAY TO GAIN LEADERSHIP:
PROBLEM SOLVING

According to F. F. Fournies, writing in *Coaching for Improved Work Performance*,[1] there are four common reasons why people do not perform the way they should:

1. They do not know *what* they are supposed to do.

2. They do not know *how* to do it.

3. They do not know *why* they should.

4. There are obstacles beyond their control.

These four reasons why people fail to perform at their potential are all responsibilities of leadership. The first three reasons deal with starting a job correctly. A training program, job description, proper tools, and vision, along with good communication skills, will go a long way in effectively meeting the first three issues.

This chapter will deal with the fourth reason that causes many people to fail to reach their performance potential. Problems continually occur at work, at home, and in life in general. My observation is that people don't like problems, weary of them quickly, and will do almost anything to get away from them. This climate makes others place the reins of leadership into your hands—*if* you are willing and able to either tackle their problems or train them to solve them. Your problem-solving skills will always be needed, because people always have problems. And when problems occur, notice where people go to solve them (see chart below).

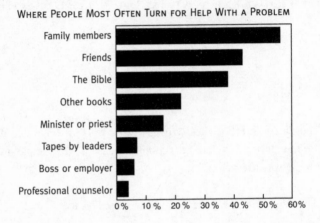

WHERE PEOPLE MOST OFTEN TURN FOR HELP WITH A PROBLEM

This chapter will deal with the two things needed to effectively solve problems: the right attitude and the right action plan.

Before these two areas are explored, I want to share with you some observations I have made about people and their problems.

WE ALL HAVE PROBLEMS

Sometimes our problems overwhelm us, as they did my friend Joe. Before Joe could get out of his house and head for work, he had four long-distance calls. Everyone seemed to have a problem. And they all wanted Joe to get on a plane that day and come help out. He finally told his wife to forget about his breakfast. He rushed out of the house as fast as he could. Then, when he stepped into the garage, he discovered his car would not start. So he called a taxi. While he was waiting for the taxi, he got another call about another problem. Finally, the taxi came and Joe rushed out, piled in the backseat, and yelled, "All right, let's get going."

> The size of the person is more important than the size of the problem.

"Where do you want me to take you?" the taxi driver asked.

"I don't care where we go," Joe shouted. "I've got problems everywhere."

Sometimes we think our generation has more problems than the last. I laughed at this idea after I reflected on the words of Dwight Bohmbach in *What's Right with America*:

> America's elders lived through the great 1929 stock market crash that ruined many of their families; the Depression years; the Bonus March on Washington, when veterans were dispersed by Army troops; the New Deal years; Pearl Harbor; the loss of the Philippines; years of long days and nights in defense plants in the 1940s; fighting in Europe and the Pacific; D-Day; the Battle of the Bulge; V-E Day; the hope-filled beginning of the United Nations in America; the A-bomb; V-J Day; the Marshall Plan in Europe; the Berlin airlift; war in Korea; the U-2 incident; the Bay of Pigs invasion; the Cuban missile crisis; the killings of President Kennedy, Bobby Kennedy, and Martin Luther King, Jr.; the civil rights struggle; the Vietnam War; Americans on the moon; Watergate and the resignation of a president and vice president; the energy crisis; Three-Mile Island; Iranian hostages; a new president shot in 1981; the bombing of our embassy and hundreds of Marines in Lebanon; becoming a debtor nation, with the highest budget deficit in history. What a lifetime!

We should remember the words of Paul Harvey, who said that in times like these it is always helpful to remember that there have always been times like these.

PROBLEMS GIVE MEANING TO LIFE

A wise philosopher once commented that an eagle's only obstacle to overcome for flying with greater speed and ease is the air. Yet, if the air were withdrawn and the proud bird were to fly in a vacuum, it would fall instantly to the ground, unable to fly at all. The very element that offers resistance to flying is at the same time the condition for flight.

> People need to change their perspectives, not their problems.

The main obstacle that a powerboat has to overcome is the water against the propeller, yet, if it were not for this same resistance, the boat would not move at all.

The same law, that obstacles are conditions of success, holds true in human life. A life free of all obstacles and difficulties would reduce all possibilities and powers to zero. Eliminate problems, and life loses its creative tension. The problem of mass ignorance gives meaning to education. The problem of ill health gives meaning to medicine. The problem of social disorder gives meaning to government.

In the South, when cotton was "king," the boll weevil crossed over from Mexico to the United States and destroyed the cotton plants. Farmers were forced to grow a variety of crops, such as soybeans and peanuts. They learned to use their land to raise cattle, hogs, and chickens. As a result, many more farmers became prosperous than in the days when the only crop grown was cotton.

The people of Enterprise, Alabama, were so grateful for what had occurred that in 1910 they erected a monument to the boll weevil. When they turned from the single-crop system to diversified farming, they became wealthier. The inscription on the monument reads: "In profound appreciation of the boll weevil and what it has done to herald prosperity."

We all have a tendency all of our lives to want to get rid of problems and responsibilities. When that temptation arises, remember the youth who was questioning a lonely old man. "What is life's heaviest burden?" he asked. The old fellow answered sadly, "Having nothing to carry."

MANY OUTSTANDING PEOPLE HAVE OVERCOME PROBLEMS IN THEIR LIVES

Many of the Psalms were born in difficulty. "Most of the Epistles were written in prisons. Most of the greatest thoughts of the greatest thinkers of all time had to pass through the fire. Bunyan wrote *Pilgrim's Progress* from jail. Florence Nightingale, too ill to move from her bed, reorganized the hospitals of England. Semiparalyzed and under constant menace of apoplexy, Pasteur was tireless in his attack on disease. During the greater part of his life, American historian Francis Parkman suffered so acutely that he could not

> Policies are many; principles are few. Policies will change; principles never do.

work for more than five minutes at a time. His eyesight was so wretched that he could scrawl only a few gigantic words on a manuscript, but he contrived to write twenty magnificent volumes of history."[2]

Bury a person in the snows of Valley Forge, and you have a George Washington. Raise him in abject poverty, and you have an Abraham Lincoln. Strike him down with infantile paralysis, and he becomes a Franklin D. Roosevelt. Burn him so severely that the doctors say he will never walk again, and you have a Glenn Cunningham, who set the world's one-mile record in 1934. Have him or her born black in a society filled with racial discrimination, and you have a Booker T. Washington, a Marian Anderson, a George Washington Carver, or a Martin Luther King Jr. Call him a slow learner and retarded—writing him off as uneducable—and you have an Albert Einstein.

Dolly Parton sums it all up with these words: "The way I see it, if you want the rainbow, you gotta put up with the rain."

MY PROBLEM IS *NOT* MY PROBLEM

There is a world of difference between a person who has a big problem and a person who makes a problem big. For several years I would do between twenty and thirty hours of counseling each week. I soon discovered that the people who came to see me were not necessarily the ones who had the most problems. They were the ones who were problem conscious and found their difficulties stressful. Naïve at first, I would try to fix their problems, only to discover that they would go out and find others. They were like Charlie Brown in a Christmas special—he just couldn't get the Christmas spirit. Linus finally said, "Charlie Brown, you're the only person I know who can take a wonderful season like Christmas and turn it into a problem."

Linus, I have news for you. There are many people like Charlie Brown! Their "problems" are not their real problems. The problem is that they react wrongly to "problems" and therefore make their "problems" real problems. What really counts is not what happens *to me* but what happens *in me*.

A study of three hundred highly successful people, people like Franklin Delano Roosevelt, Helen Keller, Winston Churchill, Albert Schweitzer, Mahatma Gandhi, and Albert Einstein, reveals that one-fourth had handicaps, such as blindness, deafness, or crippled limbs. Three-fourths had either been born in poverty, came from broken homes, or at least came from exceedingly tense or disturbed situations.

_____

Always take the
high road.

_____

Why did the achievers overcome problems, while thousands are overwhelmed by theirs? They refused to hold on to the common excuses for failure. They turned their stumbling blocks into stepping-stones. They realized they could not determine every circumstance in life, but they could determine their choice of attitude toward every circumstance.

I read about a church choir that was raising money to attend a music competition and decided to have a car wash. To their dismay, after a busy morning, rain began to pour in midafternoon, and the customers stopped coming. Finally, one of the women printed this poster: "WE WASH; [and with an arrow pointed skyward] HE RINSES!"

The *Los Angeles Times* recently ran this quote: "If you can smile whenever anything goes wrong, you are either a nitwit or a repairman." I would add: or a leader in the making—one who realizes that the only problem you have is the one you allow to be a problem because of your wrong reaction to it. Problems can stop you temporarily. You are the only one who can do it permanently.

A Problem Is Something I Can Do Something About

My friend and mentor, Fred Smith, taught me this truth. If I can't do something about a problem, it's not my problem; it's a fact of life.

In 1925, an American company manufacturing and marketing shaving cream was concerned about the effectiveness of its roadside advertising. With the introduction of "high-speed" automobiles, they were concerned that nobody had time to read their billboards. So the company, Burma Shave, created a series of small signs spaced at sufficient intervals so they could be read even at high speeds. The unique approach to advertising made Burma Shave a household name for forty-six years.

As a child growing up in Ohio, I loved the Burma Shave advertisements. This was my favorite:

> A peach looks good
> With lots of fuzz . . .
> But man's no peach . . .
> And never was.

The Burma Shave company became creative with a changing society. If there had been no answer to the problem, then there would have been no problem—just a fact of life. Be careful in resigning yourself to the position that there is no answer to a problem. Someone else may come along with a solution.

A Test of a Leader is the Ability to Recognize a Problem Before It Becomes an Emergency

Under excellent leadership a problem seldom reaches gigantic proportions, because it is recognized and fixed in its early stages.

Great leaders usually recognize a problem in the following sequence:

1. They sense it before they see it (intuition).

2. They begin looking for it and ask questions (curiosity).

3. They gather data (processing).

4. They share their feelings and findings to a few trusted colleagues (communicating).

5. They define the problem (writing).

6. They check their resources (evaluating).

7. They make a decision (leading).

Great leaders are seldom blindsided. They realize that the punch that knocks them out is seldom the hard one—it's the one they didn't see coming. Therefore, they are always looking for signs and indicators that will give them insight into the problem ahead and their odds of fixing it. They treat problems like the potential trespasser of an Indiana farm who read this sign on a fence post, "If you cross this field, you better do it in 9.8 seconds. The bull can do it in 10 seconds."

You Can Judge Leaders by the Size of the Problems They Tackle

In one of the *Peanuts* comic strips, Charlie Brown says, "There's no problem so big that I can't run from it." We all have felt exactly like the lion tamer who put this advertisement in the paper: "Lion tamer wants tamer lion."

Yet, in my observations of people and their problems, I have noticed that the size of the person is more important than the size of the problem. Problems look larger or smaller according to whether the person is large or small.

Recently, I spoke with Marcia, a lady who was diagnosed with cancer two years ago and had a mastectomy. She is doing very well. But she shared with me a concern for others who had the problem and were not doing well. There seemed to be a big difference between Marcia and others who had the same problem. I could have predicted physical recovery for Marcia. She was positive from the beginning of her problem. Our focus as a leader should be to build big people. Big people will handle big issues effectively.

SOLVE TASK PROBLEMS QUICKLY; PEOPLE PROBLEMS WILL TAKE LONGER

Solving problems may be the immediate agenda, but that should never be where we spend most of our time. If all we do is focus on solving the next problem at hand, we will soon feel like the farmer who said, "The hardest thing about milking cows is that they never stay milked." Problems never stop, but people can stop problems. My suggestion for producing problem solvers are:

1. *Make a time commitment to people.* Those who never take time to develop people are forced to take time to solve their problems.

2. *Never solve a problem for a person; solve it with that person.* Take that individual through the sequence that has already been given for recognizing a problem. In fact, spend time with that person and study this entire chapter together.

Problems should be solved at the lowest level possible. President John F. Kennedy said that President Eisenhower gave him this advice the day before his inauguration: "You'll find no easy problems ever come to the president of the United States. If they are easy to solve, somebody else has solved them." That statement should be true of every leader. Climbing the ladder of leadership means that fewer but more important decisions will be made. The problem-solving skills of a leader must be sharpened, because every decision becomes a major decision. John E. Hunter said, "A situation only becomes a problem when one does not have sufficient resources to meet it." The rest of the chapter will deal with what is needed to effectively solve problems.

THE RIGHT ATTITUDE

The subject of our attitude is so important for potential leaders that the next chapter will be given to it totally. Therefore, a few thoughts will be sufficient at this time. Norman Vincent Peale was right when he said that positive thinking is how you *think* about a problem. Enthusiasm is how you *feel* about a problem. The two together determine what you *do* about a problem. If I could do anything for people, I would help them change their perspectives, not their problems. Positive thinking does not always change our circumstances, but it will always change us. When we are able to think right about tough situations, then our journeys through life become better.

G. W. Target, in his essay "The Window," tells the story of two men confined to hospital beds in the same room. Both men were seriously ill, and though they were not allowed much diversion—no television, radio, or books—their friendship developed over months of conversation. They discussed every possible subject in which they both had interest or experience, from family to jobs to vacations, as well as much of their own personal histories.

Neither man left his bed, but one was fortunate enough to be next to the window. As part of his treatment, he could sit up in bed for just an hour a day. At this time he would describe the world outside to his roommate. In very descriptive terms he would bring the outside world inside to his friend, describing to him the beautiful park he could see, with its lake, and the many interesting people he saw spending their time there. His friend began to live for those descriptions.

After a particularly fascinating report, the one man began to think it was not fair that his friend got to see everything, while he could see nothing. He was ashamed of his thoughts, but he had quite a bit of time to think, and he couldn't get this out of his mind. Eventually his thoughts began to take their effect on his health, and he became even more ill, with a disposition to match.

One evening his friend, who sometimes had difficulty with congestion and breathing, awoke with a fit of coughing and choking and was unable to push the button for the nurse to come to his aid. The frustrated, sour man lay there looking at the ceiling, listening to this struggle for life next to him, and doing nothing.

The next morning the day nurse came in to find the man by the window dead.

After a proper interval, the man who was so eager to see out that window asked if he could be moved, and it was quickly done. As soon as the room was empty, the man struggled up on his elbow to look out the window and fill his spirit with the sights of the outside world.

It was then he discovered the window faced a blank wall.[3]

THE RIGHT ACTION PLAN

Is it not true that too many times we have a surplus of simple answers and a shortage of simple problems? Occasionally we all feel like the guy in a cartoon who said, "I try to take just one day at a time, but lately several days have attacked me at once." One thing is certain, life is not problem-free!

The story is told that when the Apollo series of space vehicles was being designed, a rift developed between the scientists and the engineers. The scientists insisted that every available ounce of weight be reserved for scientific equipment that could be used to explore and report on outer space. They wanted the engineers to design a space vehicle that would be free from all defects. (That was the era when "zero defects" was a popular expression in industry.) That would mean a large proportion of the space and weight would be available for scientific equipment.

The engineers argued that this was an impossible goal. They contended that the only safe assumption was that something would go wrong, but they could not predict with certainty where the malfunctions would occur. Therefore, they would need to build in a series of backup systems to compensate for every possible malfunction. That would mean far less weight and cargo space would be available for scientific equipment.

Allegedly this conflict was resolved by asking the astronauts in training which assumption they supported. They all voted in favor of lots of backup systems! This story illustrates the importance of assumptions. Some people assume that a defect-free system can be developed for their lives. Others assume that something will go wrong, and they need a backup system. Too many times when a problem arises, we want to blame someone else and take the easy way out. Recently I studied a humorous problem-solving chart (see opposite page) that underscores our desire to duck responsibility.

THE PROBLEM-SOLVING PROCESS

Now, even if we don't wish to duck responsibilities and we have the right attitude and a solid action plan, it is still important to follow a process when we're looking for a solution. I suggest following these steps to problem solving.

IDENTIFY THE PROBLEM

Too many times we attack the symptoms, not the cause. Ordering your staff to stay at their desks until quitting time is a Band-Aid solution that does not answer the question, "Why does the staff leave early?" Your job is to identify the real issues that lie beneath the symptoms. Failing to do this places you in the same situation as a young soldier who was learning to parachute. He was given the following instructions:

1. Jump when you are told;

2. Count to ten and pull the ripcord;

3. In the very unlikely event that it doesn't open, pull the second chute open; and

4. When you get down, a truck will take you back to the base.

PROBLEM-SOLVING FLOW CHART

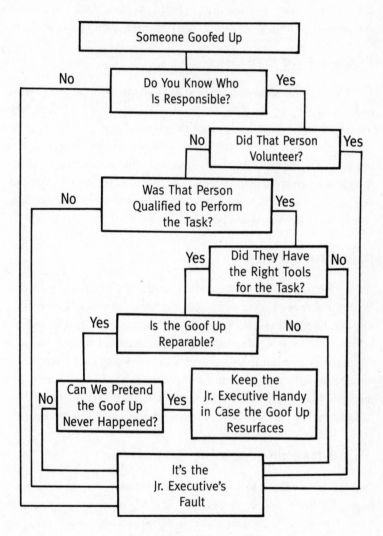

Created by David B. McGinnis

The plane got up to the proper altitude and the men started peeling out; the soldier jumped when it was his turn. He counted to ten, pulled the cord, but the chute failed to open. He proceeded to the backup plan and pulled the cord of the second chute. It, too, failed to open. "And I suppose," he complained to himself, "the truck won't be there when I get down."

PRIORITIZE THE PROBLEM

Richard Sloma says never to try to solve all the problems all at once—make them line up for you one by one. Whether you face three problems, thirty, or three hundred, "make them stand in single file so you face only one at a time." Approach these problems, not with a view of finding what you hope will be there, but to get the truth and the realities that must be grappled with. You may not like what you find. In that case, you are entitled to try to change it. But do not deceive yourself. What you do find may or may not be the real problem.

DEFINE THE PROBLEM

In a single sentence, answer the question, "What is the problem?" Bobb Biehl encourages us to keep in mind the difference between solving a problem and making a decision. A "decision is a choice you make between two or more alternatives, such as 'Should I fly to Phoenix or Chicago?' A problem is a situation that's counter to your intentions or expectations: 'I meant to fly to Chicago, but I ended up in Detroit,' or 'I meant to have $50,000 in the bank, but I'm $50,000 in the hole.'"[4]

Defining the problem in a single sentence is a *four-step process*.

1. Ask the Right Questions

If you have a vague idea, don't ask a general question, such as "What is happening here?" and don't speculate. Instead, ask process-related questions. Two words that always govern my questions are *trends* and *timing*. Most problem trails can be sniffed out if specific questions are asked in these two areas.

2. Talk to the Right People

Beware of authorities with a we-know-better attitude. These people have blind spots and are resistant to change. Creativity is essential for problem solving. In leadership conferences I often illustrate the principle by using the nine-dot problem.

Connect the nine points below with four straight lines without lifting your pen or pencil from the paper.

If you haven't encountered this problem before, try it. You were stymied if you made certain assumptions about the problem that limited your range of answers. Did you assume the lines could not extend beyond the imaginary square formed by the dots? Break that assumption and you can solve the puzzle more easily.

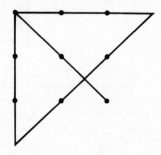

This creative solution is fairly commonplace. Less well-known are alternate solutions that stem from breaking other assumptions, such as these suggested by astronomer Tom Wujec: Assumption: The lines must pass through the center of the dots. If you draw lines that just touch the dots, you can solve the puzzle in just three strokes.

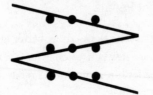

Assumption: The lines must be thin. Connect the lines with one fat line to solve this problem.

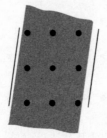

Assumption: You may not crease the paper. Fold the paper twice, so the dots all are together on the surface, and you need only one wide line.

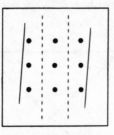

Assumption: The paper must be flat. Roll the paper into a tube. It's possible to connect the dots with a spiral.

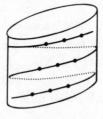

Assumption: You cannot rip the paper. Tear the paper into nine pieces with one dot on each, and connect all the dots by poking a hole through all the dots with your pencil.

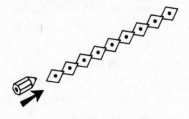

These alternate solutions make the classic nine-dot problem even more effective in conveying the message that we can find more ways to solve more problems if we break stultifying assumptions.[5]

3. Get the Hard Facts

Remember Peter Drucker's words, "Once the facts are clear, the decisions jump out at you." For example, don't let someone say to you, "That person is a good worker." Get concrete examples of that individual's performance. Listen to what is *not* being said and gather the important data.

4. Get Involved in the Process

Most problems are not what they seem. Don't just ask the right questions and gather hard facts. Get involved in the process by doing the actual jobs of the people concerned and see what problems arise. Problems should be solved at the lowest level possible, because that is where they appear. That is also the level where they are most clearly defined.

SELECT PEOPLE TO HELP YOU IN THE PROBLEM-SOLVING PROCESS

Socrates developed this method 2,400 years ago: After defining the problem at hand, he would gather others around him and ask for their opinions and logical support to back their opinions up. As self-appointed gadfly, Socrates spent most of his life causing trouble in complacent, conservative Athens. By debating, cajoling, and prodding, he forced Athenians to question beliefs they took for granted.

This finally got him into trouble. The Athenians charged him with impiety toward the gods and corrupting Athens' youth. He was thrown into prison, tried, and sentenced to death. After a month, during which he refused friends' offers to help him escape, Socrates drank a cup of hemlock and died.

Nobody expects you to go that far. But practicing the Socratic method will help you to be a better leader.[6]

Before inviting people to attend a problem-solving meeting, ask these questions:

- Is it a real problem?
- Is it urgent?
- Is the true nature of the problem known?
- Is it specific? (If people talk about everything, they will eventually talk about nothing.)
- Has the group most competent to discuss the problem been invited, and is each participant concerned about solving this issue?

COLLECT PROBLEM CAUSES

List all the possible causes of the problem by asking what caused the problem and how the problem can be avoided in the future.

COLLECT PROBLEM-SOLVING SOLUTIONS

List as many solutions to a problem as possible. The more, the better.

Seldom is there just one way to solve a problem. Options are essential because a problem continually shifts and changes. The leader without a backup solution for the primary answer will soon be in trouble.

PRIORITIZE AND SELECT THE "BEST" SOLUTIONS

Weigh all the possible solutions before deciding. The following questions should always be asked by the leader:

- Which solution has the greatest potential to be right?
- Which solution is in the best interests of the organization?
- Which solution has momentum and timing on its side?
- Which solution has the greatest chance for success?

IMPLEMENT THE BEST SOLUTION

Norman Bushnell, founder of Atari, said, "Everyone who's ever taken a shower has an idea. It's the person who gets out of the shower, dries off, and does something about it who makes a difference."

EVALUATE THE SOLUTION

Let others test it out and punch holes in it. If they punch intellectual holes (such as, "I don't think it will continue working because . . ."), ignore them. If they point out real operative problems you can observe, then you must make the adjustment. Ask these questions to evaluate the responses:

- Were we able to identify the real causes of the problem?
- Did we make the right decision?
- Has the problem been resolved?

- Have the key people accepted this solution?
- Did I help people to develop problem-solving skills to manage conflict in the future?

SET UP PRINCIPLES OR POLICIES TO KEEP PROBLEMS FROM RECURRING

Whereas policies are set up for a particular function in a specific area, principles are guidelines for everyone and are more general. Policies change when their use is no longer essential. Principles do not change.

> Policies are many,
> Principles are few,
> Policies will change,
> Principles never do.

Policies work well for lower management and operational matters. A policy should never be held on to and defended when it impedes the program and delays the change needed to make progress. A policy's intent is to give clear direction and allow a better flow in the organization. Many operational problems will stay solved with the implementation of solid policy.

A principle within my organization is: "Always take the high road." This principle means that whenever there is debate, question, tension, or confrontation between staff and people, I always expect my staff to give the benefit of the doubt to others. This principle is for everyone in my organization at all times. It may have nothing to do with an operational procedure that concerns machines and paper, but it has everything to do with people. To teach principles effectively to my staff, I must:

- model them;
- relate them by answering the question, "How can I use this in my life?"; and
- applaud when I see the principles being applied in their lives.

Later on in this book I will spend an entire chapter on the importance of having the right people around you. In regard to problem solving, if you are always the problem solver and never teach the people around you to think and decide for themselves, you will have a dependent group of followers. Many years ago I decided to focus on helping people solve problems rather than helping solve people's problems. These suggestions are some approaches you should find effective:

- Never allow others to think you always have the best answers. This will only make them dependent on you.

- Ask questions. Help people to think through the entire process of their problem.

- Become a coach, not a king. A coach brings out the best in others, helping them to reach deep down inside and discover their potential. A king only gives commands.

- List their solutions on paper. Integrate your ideas with theirs until they have ownership of them.

- Ask them to decide on the best solution to their problem.

- Develop a game plan.

- Ask them to take ownership and responsibility for the game plan. Let them set up a time frame and an accountability process.

Your goal should be that when the meeting is over, the other person has processed the problem, selected a solution, developed a game plan, and taken ownership of it. His or her relationship with you will not be a dependent one, but a deepening one.

SIX

THE EXTRA PLUS IN LEADERSHIP:
ATTITUDE

When I speak at a leadership conference, I often ask everyone to do this exercise:

Write the name of a friend whom you greatly admire:

_____

Write one thing that you admire most about that friend:

_____

I'd like you to take a moment and complete this exercise before you continue reading. I think you'll gain an interesting and important insight. The odds are high that the thing you most admire about your friend has to do with attitude. After all the conference participants have completed this exercise, I ask them to tell me their answers. I list the first twenty-five responses on an overhead projector for everyone to see. I put an A beside the characteristics that describe attitudes, an S beside those describing skills, and an L if the words deal with looks. Every time I conduct this exercise, 95 percent of the descriptive words represent attitudes for which the friends are admired.

Charles Swindoll said:

> The longer I live, the more I realize the impact of attitude on life. Attitude, to me, is more important than facts. It is more important than the past, than education, than money, than circumstances, than failures, than successes, than what other people think or say or do. It is more important than appearance, giftedness, or skill. It will make or break a company, a church, or a home. The remarkable thing is that we have a choice every day regarding the attitude we will embrace for that day. We cannot change our past. Nor can we change the fact that people will act in a certain way. We also cannot change the inevitable. The only thing that we can do is play on the one string we have, and that is our attitude. I am convinced that life is 10 percent what happens to me and 90 percent how I react to it. And so it is with you—we are in charge of our attitudes.[1]

Just as our attitudes are the extra pluses in life, they also make the difference in leading others. Leadership has less to do with position than it does with disposition. The disposition of a leader is important because it will influence the way the followers think and feel. Great leaders understand that the right attitude will set the right atmosphere, which enables the right responses from others.

OUR ATTITUDES ARE OUR MOST IMPORTANT ASSETS

Our attitude may not be the asset that makes us great leaders, but without good ones we will never reach our full potential. Our attitudes are the "and then some" that allows us the little extra edge over those whose thinking is wrong. Walt Emerson said, "What lies behind us and what lies before us are tiny matters compared to what lies within us."

The 1983 Cos Report on American Business said that 94 percent of all Fortune 500 executives attributed their success more to attitude than to any other basic ingredient.

Robert Half International, a San Francisco consulting firm, recently asked vice presidents and personnel directors at one hundred of America's largest companies to name the single greatest reason for firing an employee. The responses are very interesting and underscore the importance of attitude in the business world:

- Incompetence: 30 percent
- Inability to get along with other workers: 17 percent
- Dishonesty or lying: 12 percent
- Negative attitude: 10 percent
- Lack of motivation: 7 percent
- Failure or refusal to follow instructions: 7 percent
- All other reasons: 8 percent

Notice that although incompetence ranked first on the list, the next five were all attitude problems.

The Carnegie Institute not long ago analyzed the records of ten thousand persons and concluded that 15 percent of success is due to technical training. The other 85 percent is due to personality, and the primary personality trait identified by the research is attitude.

Our attitudes determine what we see and how we handle our feelings. These two factors greatly determine our success

What we see: Psychology 101 taught me that we see what we are prepared to see. A suburbanite, unable to find his best saw, suspected that his neighbor's son—who was always tinkering around with woodworking—had stolen it. During the next week everything the teenager did looked suspicious—the way he walked, the tone of his voice, his gestures. But when the older man found the saw behind his own workbench, where he had accidentally knocked it, he could no longer see anything at all suspicious in his neighbor's son.

Nell Mohney, in her book *Beliefs Can Influence Attitudes*, pointedly illustrates this truth. Mohney tells of a double-blind experiment conducted in the San Francisco Bay area. The principal of a school called three professors together and said, "Because you three teachers are the finest in the system and you have the greatest expertise, we're going to give you ninety high-IQ students. We're going to let you move these students through this next year at their own pace and see how much they can learn."

Everyone was delighted—faculty and students alike.

> Life is 10 percent what happens to me and 90 percent how I react to it.

Over the next year the professors and the students thoroughly enjoyed themselves. The professors were teaching the brightest students; the students were benefiting from the close attention and instruction of highly skilled teachers. By the end of the experiment, the students had achieved from 20 to 30 percent more than the other students in the whole area.

The principal called the teachers in and told them, "I have a confession to make. You did not have ninety of the most intellectually prominent students. They were run-of-the-mill students. We took ninety students at random from the system and gave them to you."

The teachers said, "This means that we are exceptional teachers."

> Leadership has less to do with position than it does disposition.

The principal continued, "I have another confession. You're not the brightest of the teachers. Your names were the first three names drawn out of a hat."

The teachers asked, "What made the difference? Why did ninety students perform at such an exceptional level for a whole year?"[2]

The difference, of course, was the teachers' expectations. Our expectations have a great deal to do with our attitudes. And these expectations may be totally false, but they will determine our attitudes.

How we handle our feelings: Notice I did not say our attitudes determine how we feel. There is a great difference between how we feel and how we handle our feelings. Everyone has times when they feel bad. Our attitudes cannot stop our feelings, but they can keep our feelings from stopping us. Unfortunately too many allow their feelings to control them until they end up like poor Ziggy in the comic strip.

> We cannot continue to function in a manner that we do not truly believe about ourselves.

He is sitting beneath a tree, gazing at the moon, and says, "I've been here and I've been there. I've been up and I've been down. I've been in and I've been out. I've been around and I've been about. But not once, not even once, have I ever been 'where it's at'!"

Every day I see people who are feeling controlled. A recent survey indicates that people with emotional problems are 144 percent more likely to have automobile accidents than those who are emotionally stable. An alarming factor revealed by this study is that one out of every five victims of fatal accidents had a quarrel within six hours before his or her accident.

IT IS IMPROBABLE THAT A PERSON WITH A BAD ATTITUDE CAN CONTINUOUSLY BE A SUCCESS

Norman Vincent Peale relates this story in his book, *Power of the Plus Factor*:

> Once walking through the twisted little streets of Kowloon in Hong Kong, I came upon a tattoo studio. In the window were displayed samples of the tattoos available. On the chest or arms you could have tattooed an anchor or flag or mermaid or whatever. But what struck me with force were three words that could be tattooed on one's flesh, *Born to lose*.
>
> I entered the shop in astonishment and, pointing to those words, asked the Chinese tattoo artist, "Does anyone really have that terrible phrase, *Born to lose*, tattooed on his body?"

> A leader's attitude is caught by his or her followers more quickly than his or her actions.

He replied, "Yes sometimes." "But," I said, "I just can't believe that anyone in his right mind would do that."

The Chinese man simply tapped his forehead and in broken English said, "Before tattoo on body, tattoo on mind."[3]

Once our minds are "tattooed" with negative thinking, our chances for long-term success diminish. We cannot continue to function in a manner that we do not truly believe about ourselves. Often I see people sabotage themselves because of wrong thinking.

The sports world has always appreciated Arnold Palmer. The members of "Arnie's army" can still be counted among young and old. This great golfer never flaunted his success. Although he has won hundreds of trophies and awards, the only trophy in his office is a battered cup that he got for his first professional win at the Canadian Open in 1955. In addition to the cup, he has a lone framed plaque on the wall. The plaque tells you why he has been so successful on and off the golf course. It reads:

If you think you are beaten, you are.
If you think you dare not, you don't.
If you'd like to win but think you can't,
It's almost certain you won't.
Life's battles don't always go
To the stronger or faster man,
But sooner or later, the man who wins
Is the man who thinks he can.

What is the difference between a golfer who wins one golf tournament and an Arnold Palmer? Is it ability? Lucky breaks? Absolutely not! When an average of less than two strokes per tournament separates the top twenty-five golfers in the world, the difference has to be something more than ability.

It's the attitude that makes the difference. People with negative thinking may start well, have a few good days, and win a match. But sooner or later (it's usually sooner), their attitude will pull them down.

WE ARE RESPONSIBLE FOR OUR ATTITUDES

Our destinies in life will never be determined by our complaining spirits or high expectations. Life is full of surprises, and the adjustment of our attitudes is a lifelong project.

> The pessimist complains about the wind.
> The optimist expects it to change.
> The leader adjusts the sails.

My father, Melvin Maxwell, has always been my hero. He is a leader's leader. One of his strengths is his positive attitude. Recently Dad and Mom spent some time with my family. As he opened his briefcase, I noticed a couple of motivational attitude books.

I said, "Dad, you're seventy years old. You've always had a great attitude. Are you still reading that stuff?"

He looked me in the eye and said, "Son, I have to keep working on my thought life. I am responsible to have a great attitude and to maintain it. My attitude does not run on automatic."

Wow! That's a lesson for all of us. We choose what attitudes we have right now. And it's a continuing choice. I am amazed at the large number of adults who fail to take responsibility for their attitudes. If they're grumpy and someone asks why, they'll say, "I got up on the wrong side of the bed." When failure begins to plague their lives, they'll say, "I was born on the wrong side of the tracks." When life begins to flatten out and others in the family are still climbing, they'll say, "Well, I was in the wrong birth order in my family." When their marriages fail, they believe they married the wrong person. When someone else gets a promotion they wanted, it's because they were in the wrong place at the wrong time.

Do you notice something? They are blaming everyone else for their problems.

The greatest day in your life and mine is when we take total responsibility for our attitudes. That's the day we truly grow up.

An advisor to President Lincoln suggested a certain candidate for the Lincoln cabinet. But Lincoln refused, saying, "I don't like the man's face."

"But, sir, he can't be responsible for his face," insisted the advisor.

"Every man over forty is responsible for his face," replied Lincoln, and the subject was dropped. No matter what you think about your attitude, it shows on your face!

The other day I saw a bumper sticker that read, "Misery is an option." I believe it! So does the daughter of a woman I heard about. The woman and her daughter went Christmas shopping together. The crowds were awful. The woman had to skip lunch because she was on a tight schedule. She became tired and hungry, and her feet were hurting. She was more than a little irritable.

As they left the last store, she asked her daughter, "Did you see the nasty look that salesman gave me?

The daughter answered, "He didn't give it to you, Mom. You had it when you went in."

> We cannot choose how many years we will live, but we can
> choose how much life those years will have.
> We cannot control the beauty of our face, but we can
> control the expression on it.
> We cannot control life's difficult moments, but we can
> choose to make life less difficult.
> We cannot control the negative atmosphere of the world,
> but we can control the atmosphere of our minds.
> Too often, we try to choose to control things we cannot.
> Too seldom, we choose to control what we can . . . our attitude.[4]

IT'S NOT WHAT HAPPENS *TO* ME THAT MATTERS BUT WHAT HAPPENS *IN* ME

Hugh Downs says that a happy person is not a person with a certain set of circumstances, but rather a person with a certain set of attitudes.

Too many people believe that happiness is a condition. When things are going great, they're happy. When things are going bad, they're sad. Some people have what I call "destination disease." They think that happiness can be found in a position or a place. Others have what I call "someone sickness." They think happiness results from knowing or being with a particular person.

I am impressed with the philosophy of the following statement: "God chooses what we go through. We choose how we go through it." It describes Viktor Frankl's attitude as he was terribly mistreated in a Nazi concentration camp. His words to his persecutors have been an inspiration to millions of people. He said, "The one thing you cannot take away from me is the way I choose to respond to what you do to me. The last of one's freedoms is to choose one's attitude in any given circumstance."[5]

Clara Barton, the founder of the American Red Cross, understood the importance of choosing a right attitude even in wrong situations. She was never known to hold a grudge against anyone. One time a friend recalled to her a cruel thing that had happened to her some years previously, but Clara seemed not to remember the incident.

"Don't you remember the wrong that was done to you?" the friend asked.

"No," Clara answered calmly. "I distinctly remember forgetting that."

Many times people who have suffered adverse situations in their lives become bitter and angry. Over time, their lives will be negative and hardened toward others. The tendency for them is to point back to a difficult time and say, "That incident ruined my life." What they do not realize is that the incident called for an attitude decision—a response. Their wrong attitude choice, not the condition, ruined their lives.

C. S. Lewis said, "Every time you make a choice you are turning the central part of you, the part that chooses, into something a little different from what it was before. And taking your life as a whole, with all your innumerable choices, you are slowly turning this central thing either into a heavenly creature or into a hellish one."[6]

THE LEADER'S ATTITUDE HELPS DETERMINE
THE ATTITUDES OF THE FOLLOWERS

Leadership is influence. People catch our attitudes just like they catch our colds—by getting close to us. One of the most gripping thoughts to ever enter my mind centers on my influence as a leader. It is important that I possess a great attitude, not only for my own success, but also for the benefit of others. My responsibilities as a leader must always be viewed in light of the many, not just myself.

Dr. Frank Crane reminds us that a ball rebounds from the wall with precisely the force with which it was thrown against the wall. There is a law in physics to the effect that action is equal to reaction. The law is also true in the realm of influence. In fact, its effects multiply with a leader's influence. The action of a leader multiplies in reaction because there are several followers. To a smile given, many smiles return. Anger unleashed toward others results in much anger returned from many. There are few actual victims of fate. The generous are helped and the stingy are shunned.

Remember the four-minute mile? People had been trying to achieve it since the days of the ancient Greeks. In fact, folklore has it that the Greeks had lions chase the runners, thinking that would make them run faster. They also tried drinking tiger's milk—not the stuff you get down at the health food store, but the real thing. Nothing they tried worked. So they decided it was impossible for a person to run a mile in four minutes or less. And for over a thousand years everyone believed it. Our bone structure is all wrong. Wind resistance is too great. We have inadequate lung power. There were a million reasons.

Then one man, one single human being, proved that the doctors, the trainers, the athletes, and the millions of runners before him who tried and failed, were all wrong. And, miracle of miracles, the year after Roger Bannister broke the four-minute mile, thirty-seven other runners broke the four-minute mile. The year after that, three hundred runners broke the four-minute mile. And a few years ago in a single race in New York, thirteen out of thirteen runners broke the four-minute mile. In other words, a few decades ago the runner who finished dead last in the New York race would have been regarded as having accomplished the impossible.

What happened? There were no great breakthroughs in training. No one discovered how to control wind resistance. Human bone structure and physiology didn't suddenly improve. But human attitudes did.

You can accomplish your goals, if you set them. Who says you're not tougher, smarter, better, harder working, more able than your competition? It does not matter if they say you can't do it. What matters, the *only* thing that matters, is if *you* say it.

Until Roger Bannister came along, we all believed the experts. And "the experts" continue to keep others from reaching their potential. Why? Because experts have influence. I believe that a leader's attitude is caught by his followers more quickly than his actions. An attitude is reflected by others even when they don't follow the action. An attitude can be expressed without a word being spoken.

The effect of a leader's attitude on others is the main reason for the importance of considering a candidate's attitude when hiring executives. Practicing psychologists list areas needing significant appraisal when employees are being considered for executive promotion: ambition; attitudes toward policy; attitudes toward colleagues; supervisory skills; and attitudes toward excessive demands on time and energy. A candidate who is out of balance in one or more of these areas would be likely to project a negative attitude and, therefore, prove to be a poor leader.

Take a moment and list the negative attitudes you possess that are influencing others right now.

1.

2.

3.

4.

HOW TO CHANGE YOUR ATTITUDE

Many people seem to suffer from what Ashley Montagu, the great Rutgers anthropologist, called *psychosclerosis*. Psychosclerosis is like arteriosclerosis, which is hardening of the arteries. Psychosclerosis is *hardening of the attitude.*

David Neiswanger of the Menninger Foundation says that if each of us can be helped by science to live a hundred years, "what will it profit us if our hates and fears, our loneliness and our remorse, will not permit us to enjoy them?"

The following sections will help you to help yourself in changing your attitude.

REVIEW

Many years ago my wife, Margaret, and I bought our first house. Our limited finances forced us to find some ways of getting what we wanted without spending a great deal of money. We agreed we would work on the front yard ourselves to save labor expenses and still create a proper setting for our home. It looked great.

One day, while I was standing in our backyard, I began to realize that we had spent no time or money making the back look good. Why? Because it couldn't be seen by others as they passed our house. We were careless about the area that was hidden.

That is exactly what people do in their personal lives. Their appearances, which can be seen outwardly, are spared no expense or energy. Yet their attitudes are neglected and underdeveloped. Remember the opening part of this chapter? Go back and read it again, and then put the necessary energy and effort into changing the inner areas of your life.

THE SIX STAGES OF ATTITUDE CHANGE

1. Identify Problem Feelings

This is the earliest stage of awareness and the easiest to declare.

2. Identify Problem Behavior

Now we go beneath the surface. What triggers wrong feelings? Write down actions that result in negative feelings.

3. Identify Problem Thinking

William James said, "That which holds our attention determines our action."

4. Identify Right Thinking

Write on paper the thinking that is right and what you desire. Because your feelings come from your thoughts, you can control your feelings by changing one thing—your thoughts!

5. Make a Public Commitment to Right Thinking

Public commitment becomes powerful commitment.

6. Develop a Plan for Right Thinking

This plan should include:

- a written definition of desired right thinking
- a way to measure progress
- a daily measuring of progress
- a person to whom you are accountable
- a daily diet of self-help materials
- associating with right-thinking people

This is a general plan for attitude self-improvement. The following steps will increase the probability of your success.

RESOLVE

Whenever a leader needs to ask others to make a commitment of time, two questions must always be answered: "Can they?" (this deals with ability) and "Will they?" (this deals with attitude). The more important question of the two is "Will they?" Two other questions usually answer the "Will they?" issue. The first is, "Is the timing right?" In other words, are the conditions right to enable positive change? The second question is, "Is their temperature hot?" Are right conditions accompanied with a red-hot desire to pay the price necessary for needed change? When both questions can be answered with a resounding Yes!, then the resolve is strong and success is possible.

REFRAME

Denis Waitley says that the winners in life think constantly in terms of I can, I will, and I am. Losers, on the other hand, concentrate their waking thoughts on what they should have done or what they didn't do. If we don't like our performances, then we must first change the picture.

Cancer researchers at King's College in London did a long-term study of fifty-seven breast cancer victims who'd had mastectomies. They found that seven out of ten women "with a fighting spirit" were alive ten years later, while four out of five women "who felt hopeless" at the diagnosis had died.

The study of hope as it affects health even has a fancy name—*psychoneuroimmunology*. Harborview Medical Center in Seattle is researching in this field, and their findings support the conclusions of the King's College researchers. In a two-year study of burn victims, the Harborview research team discovered that patients with positive attitudes recovered more quickly than those with negative ones.[7]

Reframing your attitude means:

I may not be able to change the world I see around me,
but I can change the way I see the world within me.

REENTER

As you begin changing your thinking, start immediately to change your behavior. Begin to act the part of the person you would like to become. Take action on the behavior you admire by making it your behavior. Too many people want to feel, then take action. This never works.

One day while visiting a doctor's office, I read this in a medical magazine:

> We hear it almost every day . . . sigh . . . sigh . . . sigh. "I just can't get myself motivated to lose weight, test my blood sugar, etc." And we hear an equal number of sighs from diabetes educators who can't get their patients motivated to do the right things for their diabetes and health.
>
> We have news for you. Motivation is not going to strike you like lightning. And motivation is not something that someone else— nurse, doctor, family member—can bestow or force on you. The whole idea of motivation is a trap. Forget motivation. Just do it. Exercise, lose weight, test your blood sugar, or whatever. Do it without motivation. And then, guess what? After you start doing the thing, that's when the motivation comes and makes it easy for you to keep on doing it.

"Motivation," says John Bruner, "is like love and happiness. It's a by-product. When you're actively engaged in doing something, the motivation to keep on doing it sneaks up and zaps you when you least expect it."

As Harvard psychologist Jerome Bruner says, you're more likely to act yourself into feeling than feel yourself into action. So act! Whatever it is you know you should do, do it.

The attitude development of our children, Elizabeth and Joel Porter, is very important to my wife, Margaret, and me. We learned a long time ago that the most effective way to change our children's attitudes is to work on their behaviors. But when we tell one of our children, "Change your attitude," the message is too general and the change we want is unclear. A more effective approach is explaining behaviors that signify bad attitudes. If we help them change their behaviors, the attitudes will change on their own. Instead of saying to our kids, "Get a grateful attitude," we ask them to give one compliment to every member of the family each day. As this becomes a habit in their lives, the attitude of gratitude follows.

REPEAT

Paul Meier said, "Attitudes are nothing more than habits of thought, and can be acquired. An action repeated becomes an attitude realized." Once, while leading a conference, I was asked for a simple plan to help a person change some wrong attitudes. I recommended two things to help her change her attitude. First:

> Say the right words,
> Read the right books,
> Listen to the right tapes,
> Be with the right people,
> Do the right things,
> Pray the right prayer.

The second was to do number one every day, not just once or only when you feel like it, and watch your life change for the better.

RENEWAL

Fortunately, over a period of time a positive attitude can replace a negative one. Again, let me emphasize that the battle is never over, but it is well worth our efforts. The more that negative thoughts are weeded out and replaced by positive ones, the more personal renewal will be experienced. My friend Lena Walker wrote a tribute about her grandfather and a practice in his life that he passed on to her. These words effectively describe the ongoing process of attitude development and the worthiness of overcoming negative thinking.

Each year as spring approaches, my thoughts turn to a white-haired old man who went forth at this time of year to do battle. The enemy was not flesh and blood, but a small yellow flower called "mustard." As one gazes out over the fields and meadows, this yellow touch seems harmless enough, but year by year it continues its march, and can eventually take over entire fields.

Each spring my grandfather would walk through his fields, pulling these yellow flowers out by the roots.

Eventually I was married and lived on a farm in Ohio. Each spring I, too, would look out and see these same yellow flowers. The first few years on the farm I did nothing about them, but as maturity came upon me, I could see the wisdom of my grandfather's efforts. I, too, decided to go forth as he had done and do battle with the enemy.

Now, each year I walk through the fields, pulling an occasional mustard plant, I feel I am doing it in tribute to my grandfather.

To me this weed represents our bad habits and negative thoughts. We need to constantly prune out these things so our lives can be lush and green in our quest for a happy and productive life.

SEVEN

DEVELOPING YOUR MOST APPRECIABLE ASSET:
PEOPLE

The one who influences others to follow only is a leader with certain limitations. The one who influences others to lead others is a leader without limitations. As Andrew Carnegie said, no man will make a great leader who wants to do it all himself or to get all the credit for doing it.

Guy Ferguson puts it this way:

> To know how to do a job is the accomplishment of labor;
> To be available to tell others is the accomplishment of the teacher;
> To inspire others to do better work is the accomplishment of management;
> To be able to do all three is the accomplishment of true leaders.

This chapter will focus on the importance of developing people to share in and assist you with the implementation of your dreams as a leader. The thesis is: *The more people you develop, the greater the extent of your dreams.*

People who are placed in leadership positions, but attempt to do it all alone, will someday come to the same conclusion as the bricklayer who tried to move five hundred pounds of bricks from the top of a four-story building to the sidewalk below. His problem was that he tried to do it alone. On an insurance claim form, he explained what happened: "It would have taken too long to carry the bricks down by hand, so I decided to put them in a barrel and lower them by a pulley that I had fastened to the top of the building. After tying the rope securely at the ground level, I then went up to the top of the building. I fastened the rope around the barrel, loaded it with bricks, and swung it out over the sidewalk for the descent.

"Then I went down to the sidewalk and untied the rope, holding it securely to guide the barrel down slowly. But, since I weigh only one hundred and forty pounds, the five-hundred-pound load jerked me from the ground so fast I didn't have time to think of letting go of the rope. And as I passed between the second and third floors, I met the barrel coming down. This accounts for the bruises and lacerations on my upper body.

"I held tightly to the rope until I reached the top, where my hand became jammed in the pulley. This accounts for my broken thumb. At the same time, however, the barrel hit the sidewalk with a bang, and the bottom fell out. With the weight of the bricks gone, the barrel weighed only about forty pounds. Thus, my one-hundred-forty-pound body began a swift descent, and I met the empty barrel coming up. This accounts for my broken ankle.

"Slowed only slightly, I continued the descent and landed on the pile of bricks. This accounts for my sprained back and broken collarbone.

"At this point, I lost my presence of mind completely and let go of the rope. And the empty barrel came crashing down on me. This accounts for my head injuries.

"As for the last question on the form, 'What would you do if the same situation arose again?' please be advised that I am finished trying to do the job alone."

I have observed that there are three levels of people/work skills:

Level 1: The person who works better with people is a follower.
Level 2: The person who helps people work better is a manager.
Level 3: The person who develops better people to work is a leader.

PRINCIPLES FOR PEOPLE DEVELOPMENT

My success in developing others will depend on how well I accomplish each of the following:

- **Value of people.** This is an issue of my attitude.
- **Commitment to people.** This is an issue of my time.
- **Integrity with people.** This is an issue of my character.
- **Standard for people.** This is an issue of my vision.
- **Influence over people.** This is an issue of my leadership.

From my own experience and through observation of other leaders who excel in this vital area, I have discovered that there are three areas in which successful people developers are different from those who are not successful in developing others. Successful people developers:

1. make the right assumptions about people;

2. ask the right questions about people; and

3. give the right assistance to people.

SUCCESSFUL PEOPLE DEVELOPERS
MAKE THE RIGHT ASSUMPTIONS ABOUT PEOPLE

Motivating others has always been relatively easy for me. For years I was asked, "John, how do you motivate people?" My pat answers were things like, "Stay enthusiastic"; "encourage others"; "lead the way"; "believe in people." I would watch others follow my advice and be successful for a short time, only to fall back into the old habit patterns and the resulting low morale.

Observing this downward cycle, I would ask myself why the people who took my advice couldn't continually motivate others. Then one day it hit me! I was giving them the *fruit* of my motivational gifts, but not the *root*. They were writing down my outward answers without the benefit of my inward assumptions about people. My assumptions about others are what allow me to continually motivate and develop them. In fact, a leader's having the right assumptions about people is the key factor in their continual development.

> The one who influences others to lead is a leader without limitations.

An assumption is an opinion that something is true. My assumptions about people largely determine how I treat them. Why? What I assume about people is what I look for. What I look for is what I find. What I find influences my response. Therefore, negative assumptions about others will stimulate negative leadership of them. Positive assumptions about others will stimulate positive leadership of them. Here are several such assumptions about people that I have found to be extremely valuable.

ASSUMPTION: EVERYONE WANTS TO FEEL WORTHWHILE

The most successful teachers, writers, managers, politicians, philosophers, and leaders who deal with people instinctively know this simple fact: Every person in the world is hungry. Yes, every person in this world is hungry for something, be it recognition, companionship, understanding, love—the list is endless. One thing I always find on a list of people's needs is the desire to feel worthwhile. People want to feel important! Donald Laird says to always help people increase their own self-esteem. Develop your skills in making other people feel important. There is hardly a higher compliment you can pay an individual than to help that person be useful and find satisfaction and significance. I believe that!

My travel schedule is heavy, and often I stop in the terminal in San Diego to get my shoes shined. Melvin, the man who shines my shoes, has become a friend. As we talk, I always try to bring two things into the conversation. I inquire about the Little League team he coaches, because that is the love of his life. And then I tell him, and anyone else who might be listening, that Melvin can polish shoes better than anyone I've ever known.

Napoleon Bonaparte, a leader's leader, knew every officer of his army by name. He liked to wander through his camp, meet an officer, greet him by name, and talk about a battle or maneuver he knew this officer had been involved in. He never missed an opportunity to inquire about a soldier's hometown, wife, and family; the men were always amazed to see how much detailed personal information about each one the emperor was able to store in his memory.

Since every officer felt Napoleon's personal interest in him—proved by his statements and questions—it is easy to understand the devotion they all felt for him.

ASSUMPTION: EVERYONE NEEDS AND RESPONDS TO ENCOURAGEMENT

For twenty-three years I have been responsible for developing people. I have yet to find a person who did not do better work and put forth greater effort under a spirit of approval than under a spirit of criticism. Encouragement is oxygen to the soul.

Researchers are turning up new evidence to support the old truth that encouragement brings out the best in people. In one experiment, adults were given ten puzzles to solve. All ten were exactly the same for all the adults. They worked on them and turned them in and were given results at the end. However, the results were fictitious. Half of the exam takers were told they had done well, getting seven of ten correct. The other half were told they had done poorly, getting seven of ten wrong. Then all were given another ten puzzles. Again, the puzzles were the same for each person. The half who had been told they had done well with the first puzzles did better with the second set. The other half did worse.[1] Criticism, even though it was given falsely, ruined them.

Viktor Frankl said:

> If you treat people to a vision of themselves, if you apparently overrate them, you make them become what they are capable of becoming. You know, if we take people as they are, we make them worse. If we take them as they should be, we help them become what they can be. . . . If you say this is idealism—overrating man—then I must answer, "Idealism is the real realism, because you help people actualize themselves."[2]

Take a moment and link the definition of leadership (influence) with the responsibility of leadership (people development). How do we who influence others truly motivate and develop them? We do it through encouragement and belief in them. People tend to become what the most important people in their lives think they will become. I try to model and then encourage my staff to say something uplifting to others in the first sixty seconds of a conversation. That sets a positive tone for everything else.

> People tend to become what the most important people in their lives think they will become.

In describing what makes a great baseball manager, Reggie Jackson said that a great manager has a knack for making ballplayers think they are better than they are. He forces you to have a good opinion of yourself. He lets you know he believes in you. He makes you get more out of yourself. And once you learn how good you really are, you never settle for playing anything less than your best.

Henry Ford said, "My best friend is the one who brings out the best in me." How true. Every leader wants to bring out the best that is in people. And every successful leader knows that encouragement is the way to do it.

ASSUMPTION: PEOPLE "BUY INTO" THE LEADER BEFORE THEY "BUY INTO" HIS OR HER LEADERSHIP

Too often we expect people to be loyal to the position of a leader instead of the person who occupies that position. But people are not motivated by organizational charts; they respond to people. The first thing a leader must declare is not authority because of rights, but authority because of relationships. People do not care how much you know until they know how much you care. You've got to give loyalty down before you receive loyalty up. If people do not believe in their leader, anything will hinder them from following. If people believe in their leader, nothing will stop them.

> People do not care how much you know until they know how much you care.

Most of us think of Christopher Columbus as a great discoverer, but he was also a great leader and salesman. Before he could begin his voyage of discovery that changed the world, he had to sell what, to his contemporaries, was an utterly ridiculous idea! And that was no "one call" sale! Consider the circumstances and conditions that were stacked against him.

First, there was absolutely no market for a transatlantic voyage. And hundreds of years of tradition and superstition practically guaranteed there never would be.

Second, although Columbus had made sea voyages as a passenger, he had never been the captain of a ship.

Third, Columbus was a foreigner (an Italian) living in Portugal and then in Spain.

Fourth, Columbus did not have sufficient money to fund such an adventure. In fact, the only one who could legally fund a voyage of discovery was a head of state—a king or a queen. So his prospect list of benefactors was rather short.

Fifth, his price was not cheap. In addition to needing ships and support, Columbus had a long list of personal demands, including: (a) a 10 percent commission on all commerce between his discoveries and the mother country; (b) a title—Admiral of the Ocean Sea; (c) the permanent position of governor of all new territories; and (d) all of his honors and rights passed on to his heirs.

Remarkably, Columbus made the sale and did it on his own terms! Modern salespeople could learn a lot from Columbus's sales techniques.

He was propelled by a single-minded passion. He wholeheartedly believed he could reach Asia by crossing the Atlantic. Even though his belief was wrong, it gave him the stamina, conviction, and confidence to convince others. And he never stopped selling.

He didn't mind asking for the order again and again and again! He spent seven years asking King John of Portugal to fund the voyage. Then he went to Spain and worked on Ferdinand and Isabella for seven years before he finally got his Yes.

Columbus had to see before he could sail. Any successful leader knows this truth. People must buy into you before they buy into your dreams. High morale in an organization comes from having faith in the person at the top.

ASSUMPTION: MOST PEOPLE DO NOT KNOW HOW TO BE SUCCESSFUL

Most people think success is luck, and they keep trying to win the lottery of life. But success is really the result of planning. It happens where preparation and opportunity meet.

Most people think success is instantaneous. They look at it as a moment, an event, or a place in time. It's not. Success is really a process. It is growth and development. It is achieving one thing and using that as a stepping-stone to achieve something else. It is a journey.

> Failure is the opportunity to begin again more intelligently.

Most people think that success is learning how to never fail. But that's not true. Success is learning from failure. Failure is the opportunity to begin again more intelligently. Failure only truly becomes failure when we do not learn from it.

Once people realize that you, as a leader, can help them become successful, they're yours! Someone said, "Success is relative. Once you have it, all the relatives come." This is also true in an organization. Once the leader has proven to be successful and shown an interest in helping others achieve success through the company, that leader will have loyal followers who are willing to develop and grow.

ASSUMPTION: MOST PEOPLE ARE NATURALLY MOTIVATED

Just watch a one-year-old try to explore and find out what is in a house. That is natural motivation. My observation is that people begin an endeavor with a desire to participate, but are often de-motivated and then must be re-motivated to participate.

Little children want to go to school. Three- and four-year-old children "play" school. They can't wait to begin. They start off in first grade with shiny new lunch boxes and a high degree of motivation. However, by the time they are in school for two or three years, some kids hate it. They make excuses not to go, complaining, "I have a sore tummy." What happened? The schools effectively de-motivated the original high degree of enthusiasm and excitement.

The true secret of motivation is creating an environment in which people are free from the influences that demotivate.

What Motivates People?

Significant contributions. People want to join in a group or pursue a cause that will have lasting impact. They need to see that what they are doing is not wasted effort, but is making a contribution. People must see value in what they are doing. Motivation comes not by activity alone, but by the desire to reach the end result.

Goal participation. People support what they create. Being part of the goal-setting process is motivating, and it allows people to feel needed. They like to feel they are making a difference. When people have given input, they have a stake in the issue. They own it and support it. Seeing goals become reality and helping to shape the future is fulfilling. Goal participation builds team spirit, enhances morale, and helps everyone feel important.

Positive dissatisfaction. Someone said that *dissatisfaction* is the one-word definition for *motivation*. Dissatisfied people are highly motivated people, for they see the need for immediate change. They know something is wrong and often know what needs to be done. Dissatisfaction can inspire change or it can lead to a critical spirit. It can lead to apathy or stir one to action. The key is harnessing this energy toward effective change.

Recognition. People want to be noticed. They want credit for personal achievements and appreciation for their contributions. Often, giving recognition is another way of saying thanks. Personal accomplishment is motivating, but it is much more so when someone notices the accomplishment and gives worth to it. Recognition is one way to give meaning to a person's existence.

Clear expectations. People are motivated when they know exactly what they are to do and have the confidence that they can do it successfully. No one wants to jump into a task that is vague or a job whose description is uncertain. Motivation rises in a job when the goals, expectations, and responsibilities are clearly understood. When delegating responsibility, be sure to give the necessary authority to carry out the task. People perform better when they have some control over their work and their time.

What Demotivates People?

Certain behavior patterns can be demotivating. We sometimes behave in these ways without realizing the negative influences they have on others. Here's how we can avoid demotivating behavior.

Don't belittle anyone. Public criticism and cutting conversations, even in jest, can hurt. We must be alert and sensitive. Taken to the extreme, belittling can destroy a person's self-esteem and self-confidence. If you have to give criticism, remember that it takes nine positive comments to balance one negative correction.

Don't manipulate anyone. No one likes to feel maneuvered or used. Manipulation, no matter how slight, tears down the walls of trust in a relationship. We gain more by being honest and transparent than we do by being cunning and crafty. Build people up through affirmation and praise, and they'll be motivated and loyal. Remember, give and it shall be given to you.

Don't be insensitive. Make people your priority. People are our greatest resources; therefore, take time to know and care about them. This means being responsive in conversation, never appearing preoccupied with self or in a hurry. Stop talking and develop the art of really listening. Quit thinking of what you will say next, and begin to hear, not only what they say, but how they feel. Your interest in even insignificant matters will demonstrate your sensitivity.

Don't discourage personal growth. Growth is motivating, so encourage your staff to stretch. Give them opportunities to try new things and acquire new skills. We should not feel threatened by the achievements of others, but should be very supportive of their successes. Allow your staff to succeed and fail. Build the team spirit approach that says, "If you grow, we all benefit."

SUCCESSFUL PEOPLE DEVELOPERS ASK THE RIGHT QUESTIONS ABOUT PEOPLE

Now we have completed the discussion of how making the right assumptions about people must be our first principle to follow as a successful people developer. Next we need to become familiar with the right questions to ask people. There are six.

AM I BUILDING PEOPLE, OR AM I BUILDING MY DREAM AND USING PEOPLE TO DO IT?

People must come first. Fred Smith says that Federal Express, from its inception, has put its people first because it is right to do so and because it is good business as well. "Our corporate philosophy is succinctly stated: People-Service-Profits."

This question deals with the leader's motives. There is a slight but significant difference between manipulation and motivation.

Manipulation is moving together for *my* advantage.

Motivation is moving together for *mutual* advantage.

Do I Care Enough to Confront People When It Will Make a Difference?

Confrontation is very difficult for most people. If you feel uneasy just reading the word *confront*, I'd like to suggest that you substitute the word *clarify*. Clarify the issue instead of confronting the person. Then follow these ten commandments.

The Ten Commandments of Confrontation

1. Do it privately, not publicly.

2. Do it as soon as possible. That is more natural than waiting a long time.

3. Speak to one issue at a time. Don't overload the person with a long list of issues.

4. Once you've made a point, don't keep repeating it.

5. Deal only with actions the person can change. If you ask the person to do something he or she is unable to do, frustration builds in your relationship.

6. Avoid sarcasm. Sarcasm signals that you are angry at people, not at their actions, and may cause them to resent you.

7. Avoid words like *always* and *never*. They usually detract from accuracy and make people defensive.

8. Present criticisms as suggestions or questions if possible.

9. Don't apologize for the confrontational meeting. Doing so detracts from it and may indicate you are not sure you had the right to say what you did.

10. Don't forget the compliments. Use what I call the "sandwich" in these types of meetings: Compliment—Confront—Compliment.

AM I LISTENING TO PEOPLE WITH MORE THAN MY EARS, THAT IS, AM I HEARING MORE THAN WORDS?

The following test is one I have found useful and have given to my own staff.

Am I a Good Listener?

Give yourself four points if the answer to the following questions is *Always*: three points for *Usually*; two points for *Rarely*; and one point for *Never*.

_____ Do I allow the speaker to finish without interrupting?

_____ Do I listen "between the lines," that is, for the subtext?

_____ When writing a message, do I listen for and write down the key facts and phrases?

_____ Do I repeat what the person just said to clarify the meaning?

_____ Do I avoid getting hostile and/or agitated when I disagree with the speaker?

_____ Do I tune out distractions when listening?

_____ Do I make an effort to seem interested in what the other person is saying?

Scoring:

26 or higher: You are an excellent listener.

22–25: Better than average score.

18–21: Room for improvement.

17 or lower: Get out there right away and practice your listening.[3]

David Burns, a medical doctor and professor of psychiatry at the University of Pennsylvania, says: "The biggest mistake you can make in trying to talk convincingly is to put your highest priority on expressing your ideas and feelings. What most people really want is to be listened to, respected, and understood. The moment people see that they are being understood, they become more motivated to understand your point of view."

WHAT ARE THE MAJOR STRENGTHS OF THIS INDIVIDUAL?

Anyone who continually has to work in areas of personal weakness instead of personal strengths will not stay motivated. If individuals have been grinding away at tasks assigned in their weak areas and you reassign them to work in areas of strength, you'll see a dramatic increase in natural motivation.

HAVE I PLACED A HIGH PRIORITY ON THE JOB?

People tend to stay motivated when they see the importance of the things they are asked to do. The five most encouraging words in an organization are: "It will make a difference." The five most discouraging words in an organization are: "It won't make any difference."

I can still remember the day Linda was hired to oversee the computer system in our offices. She came into my office for an initial meeting. My goal was to give her the big picture to help her see that her work was more than computers. I conveyed that doing her job with excellence would encourage every worker to do a better job. I can still see her eyes moisten as she realized that her work would positively contribute to everyone's success.

HAVE I SHOWN THE VALUE THE PERSON WILL RECEIVE FROM THIS RELATIONSHIP?

People tend to stay motivated when they see the value to them of the things they are asked to do. The simple fact is when we hear an announcement, see a commercial, or are asked to make a commitment, a small voice in the back of our minds asks, "What's in it for me?" The reason people skip the meeting you worked so hard to plan is simple: they haven't seen the value (benefits and rewards) they will receive by being there.

Think about an important relationship you have with a subordinate or perhaps with your boss. On the left-hand side of a page, draw up a list of all the contributions you are making to this relationship, that is, what you are giving. With a subordinate, your list might include pay, job security, time, and professional development. Title this list "What I Give."

On the right-hand side of the page, make a second list, entitled "What I Get." Write all the benefits you are receiving. Then sit back and compare your two lists. Don't count the number of items on each one. (Some things are more important than others, and you probably left some items off both lists.) Instead, answer this simple question: *Considering all that you give to your relationship versus all that you're getting from it, who is getting the better deal?* Choose your answer from the following options:

1. *I am getting a better deal.* This can produce complacency and ingratitude.

2. *The other person is getting a better deal.* This can produce resentment.

3. *We are getting an equally good deal.* This usually produces mutual respect and motivation.

Analyze your answer by looking at the three axioms of the Equity Factor (found in Huseman and Hatfield's *Managing the Equity Factor*):

1. People evaluate relationships by comparing what they give to a relationship with what they get from it.

2. When what people give does not equal what they get, they feel distress.

3. People who feel distress because they give more than they get will restore equity. This becomes a negative. Do you commit here?[4]

SUCCESSFUL PEOPLE DEVELOPERS GIVE THE RIGHT ASSISTANCE TO PEOPLE

I need to work out their strengths and work on their weaknesses. The question that as a leader I must continually ask is not, "How hard does this person work?" (Is he or she faithful?) but "How much does this person accomplish?" (Is he or she fruitful?).

Some of the most capable people in an organization never utilize their greatest strengths. They may be locked into what management considers important jobs, and they may do them well. But they may never get an opportunity to do what they can do best. When this happens, everybody loses. The person loses because of lack of opportunity and lack of job satisfaction; the organization loses because it wastes some of its most valuable assets. The whole venture operates at less than capacity.

I must give them myself. You can *impress* people at a distance, but you can only *impact* them up close.

- List all the people you spent thirty minutes with this week.

- Did you initiate the time or did they?

- Did you have an agenda before the meeting?

- Was the meeting for the purpose of relationships, counseling, communication, or development?

- Was it a win-win meeting?

- Was it with the influential top 20 or the lower 80 percent?

Love everyone, but give yourself to the top 20 percent in your organization. Encourage the many; mentor the few. Be transparent with them. Develop a plan for their growth. Become a team.

I must give them ownership. As Sidney J. Harris believes:

People want to be appreciated, not impressed.
They want to be regarded as human beings,
Not as sounding boards for other people's egos.
They want to be treated as an end in themselves,
Not as a means toward the gratification of another's vanity.

I must give them every chance for success. My responsibility as a leader is to provide assistance for those who work with me by giving them:

- An excellent atmosphere to work in. It should be positive, warm, open, creative, and encouraging.

- The right tools to work with. Do not hire excellent people to do excellent work with average tools.

- A continual training program to work under. Growing employees make growing companies.

- Excellent people to work for. Develop a team. Coming together is the beginning. Working together is success.

- A compelling vision to work toward. Allow your people to work for something larger than themselves.

Great leaders always give their people a head start over those who work under an average leader. Excellent leaders add value to their people and help them become better than they would be if they worked alone. The first question a leader should ask is: "How can I help make those around me more successful?" When that answer is found and implemented, everyone wins!

PEOPLE-DEVELOPMENT PRINCIPLES

PEOPLE DEVELOPMENT TAKES TIME

At one time Andrew Carnegie was the wealthiest man in America. He came to America from his native Scotland when he was a small boy, did a variety of odd jobs, and eventually ended up as the largest steel manufacturer in the United States. At one time he had forty-three millionaires working for him. In those days, a millionaire was a rare person; conservatively speaking, a million dollars in his day would be equivalent to at least twenty million dollars today.

A reporter asked Carnegie how he hired forty-three millionaires. Carnegie responded that those men were not millionaires when they started working for him but had become millionaires as a result.

The reporter then asked how he had developed these men to become so valuable that he would pay them so much money.

Carnegie replied that men are developed the same way gold is mined. When gold is mined, several tons of dirt must be moved to get an ounce of gold, but one doesn't go into the mine looking for dirt. One goes in looking for gold.

Robert Half said, "There is something that is much more scarce, something rarer than ability. It is the ability to recognize ability." There is still another step that must be taken beyond the ability to discover the gold that is in the leader's mine. It must also be developed. It is better to train ten people to work than to do the work of ten people, but it is harder. "The man who goes alone can start the day. But he who travels with another must wait until the other is ready."[5]

PEOPLE SKILLS ARE ESSENTIAL FOR SUCCESS

Companies that go along successfully have leaders who get along with people. Dave E. Smalley records in his book, *Floorcraft*, that Andrew Carnegie once paid Charles Schwab a salary of one million dollars a year simply because Schwab got along with the people. Carnegie had men who understood the job better and who were better fitted by experience and training to execute it, but they lacked the essential human quality of being able to get others to help them—to get the best out of the workers.

Most chief executives of major companies, when asked what one single characteristic is most needed by those in leadership positions, replied, "The ability to work with people."

Teddy Roosevelt said, "The most important single ingredient to the formula of success is knowing how to get along with people."

John Rockefeller, who built giant corporations, stated that he would pay more for the ability to deal with people than any other ability under the sun.

The Center for Creative Leadership in Greensboro, North Carolina, studied 105 successful executives and discovered the following:

- They admitted their mistakes and accepted the consequences, rather than trying to blame others.
- They were able to get along with a wide variety of people.
- They had strong interpersonal skills, sensitivity to others, and tact.
- They were calm and confident, rather than moody and volatile.

Unsuccessful executives tended to be too tough, abusive, sarcastic, aloof, or unpredictable. Their worst fault was being insensitive to others.

Lack of people skills can result in the kind of situation former Denver Bronco coach John Ralston experienced when he left the team. "I left because of illness and fatigue—the fans were sick and tired of me."

BE A MODEL THAT OTHERS CAN FOLLOW

The number one motivational principle in the world is: *People do what people see.* The speed of the leader determines the speed of the followers. And followers will never go any further than their leader. For years I have followed and taught this process for developing others:

ACTION	RESULT
I do it:	I model.
I do it, and you are with me:	I mentor.
You do it, and I am with you:	I monitor.
You do it:	You move forward.
You do it, and someone is with you:	We multiply.

People's minds are changed more through observation than through arguments.

Benjamin Franklin learned that plaster scattered in the fields would make things grow. He told his neighbors, but they did not believe him. They argued with him, trying to prove that plaster could be of no use at all to grass or grain. After a little while he allowed the matter to drop and said no more about it.

Early the next spring Franklin went into the field and sowed some grain. Close by the path, where men would walk, he traced some letters with his finger, put plaster into them, and then sowed seed in the plaster. After a week or two the seed sprang up.

As they passed that way, the neighbors were very surprised to see, in brighter green than all the rest of the field, large letters saying, "This has been plastered." Benjamin Franklin did not need to argue with his neighbors anymore about the benefits of plaster for the field.

LEAD OTHERS BY LOOKING THROUGH THEIR EYES

Henry Wadsworth Longfellow said, "We judge ourselves by what we feel capable of doing; while others judge us by what we have already done."

Any leader who successfully deals with a group of people realizes that they each have their own agenda and perception of how things are. Long ago I learned that people think their:

> problems are the biggest,
> children are the smartest,

jokes are the funniest, and
faults ought to be overlooked.

An amusing story beautifully illustrates how each of us views life.

After World War II, a general and his young lieutenant boarded a train in England. The only seats left were across from a beautiful young lady and her grandmother. The general and the lieutenant sat facing the women. As the train pulled out, it went through a long tunnel. For about ten seconds there was total darkness. In the silence of the moment, those on the train heard two things—a kiss and a slap. Everyone on the train had his or her own perception of what happened.

The young lady thought to herself, *I'm flattered that the lieutenant kissed me, but I'm terribly embarrassed that Grandmother hit him!*

The Grandmother thought, *I'm aggravated that the young man kissed my granddaughter, but I'm proud she had the courage to retaliate!*

The general sat there, thinking to himself, *My lieutenant showed a lot of guts in kissing that girl, but why did she slap me by mistake?*

The lieutenant was the only one on the train who really knew what happened. In that brief moment of darkness, he had the opportunity to kiss a pretty girl *and* slap his general.[6]

These questions will help you discover another person's agenda in a variety of situations:

- Background question: What is this person's history with this organization or another?

- Temperament question: What is this person's primary and secondary temperament?

- Security question: Is this, in any way, affecting the individual's job?

- Relationship question: How is he or she related to me, or someone else, organizationally?

- Motive question: What is the real reason this is on his or her agenda?

- Potential question: Does this person or issue merit the leader's time and energy?

I have discovered that the development of people is more successful when I:

>listen well enough to lead through their eyes;
>relate well enough to communicate with their hearts:
>work well enough to place tools in their hands;
>think well enough to challenge and expand their minds.

LEADERS MUST CARE FOR PEOPLE BEFORE THEY CAN DEVELOP THEM

Too often I see leaders who request commitment from people without showing them proper care. They are like Narvaez, the Spanish patriot who, while dying, was asked by his father-confessor whether he had forgiven all his enemies. Narvaez looked astonished and said, "Father, I have no enemies. I shot them all."

Narvaez didn't know that "nice guys" get the best results from subordinates. Teleometrics International studied the perception high-achieving executives have of the people in their organizations, compared to low-achieving executives. Their results were reported in the *Wall Street Journal*.

Of the sixteen thousand executives studied, the 13 percent identified as "high achievers" tended to care about people as well as profits. Average achievers concentrated on production, while low achievers were preoccupied with their own security. High achievers viewed subordinates optimistically, while low achievers showed a basic distrust of subordinates' abilities. High achievers sought advice from their subordinates; low achievers didn't. High achievers were listeners; moderate achievers listened only to superiors; low achievers avoided communication and relied on policy manuals.

PEOPLE DEVELOPERS LOOK FOR OPPORTUNITIES TO BUILD UP PEOPLE

Most people in leadership positions daily steal someone's ego food—the satisfaction of their needs for esteem. In fact, they steal it and don't even know it. For example, someone says, "I've really had a busy day," and the leader replies, "You've been busy! You should see all the work piled on my desk, and I can't even get to it." Or someone says, "I finally finished that project I've been working on for eight months," and the leader replies, "Yeah, Jim finally finished that big project he's been working on too."

What is the leader doing? Well, he's taking away the food that people need for their ego. In effect, he's saying, "You may think you're pretty good, but let me tell you about someone else who is probably better."

Just for fun, check yourself tomorrow and see how many times you catch yourself satisfying your own esteem needs by stealing away someone else's ego food.

J. C. Staehle, after analyzing many surveys, found that the principal causes of unrest among workers are actions good leaders can avoid. They are listed in the order of their importance.

1. Failure to give credit for suggestions

2. Failure to correct grievances

3. Failure to encourage

4. Criticizing employees in front of other people

5. Failure to ask employees their opinions

6. Failure to inform employees of their progress

7. Favoritism

Note: Every issue is an example of the leader stealing or keeping ego food from the workers.

THE GREATEST POTENTIAL FOR GROWTH OF A COMPANY IS GROWTH OF ITS PEOPLE

In a survey of workers across the United States, nearly 85 percent said they could work harder on the job. More than half claimed they could double their effectiveness "if [they] wanted to."[7]

People are the principal asset of any company, whether it makes things to sell, sells things made by other people, or supplies intangible services. Nothing moves until your people can make it move. In actual studies of leadership in American business, the average executive spends three-fourths of his working time dealing with *people*. The largest single cost in most business is *people*. The largest, most valuable asset any company has is its *people*. All executive plans are carried out, or fail to be carried out, by *people*.

According to William J. H. Boetcker, people divide themselves into four classes:

1. Those who always do less than they are told

2. Those who will do what they are told, but no more

3. Those who will do things without being told

4. Those who will inspire others to do things

It's up to you.

As Ralph Waldo Emerson said, "Trust men and they will be true to you: treat them greatly and they will show themselves great."

Some of the best advice you can find about being a good leader is found in this old Chinese poem:

> Go to the people,
> Live among them.
> Learn from them.
> Love them.
> Start with what they know,
> Build on what they have.
> But of the best leaders,
> When their task is accomplished,
> Their work is done,
> The people will remark,
> "We have done it ourselves."

EIGHT

THE INDISPENSABLE QUALITY OF LEADERSHIP:
VISION

Robert K. Greenleaf, in his book, *The Servant as Leader*, says, "Foresight is the 'lead' that the leader has. Once he loses this lead and events start to force his hand, he is leader in name only. He is not leading; he is reacting to immediate events, and he probably will not long be a leader. There are abundant current examples of loss of leadership which stem from a failure to foresee what reasonably could have been foreseen, and from failure to act on that knowledge while the leader has freedom to act."[1]

My observation over the last twenty years has been that all effective leaders have a vision of what they must accomplish. That vision becomes the energy behind every effort and the force that pushes through all the problems. With vision, the leader is on a mission and a contagious spirit is felt among the crowd until others begin to rise alongside the leader. Unity is essential for the dream to be realized. Long hours of labor are given gladly to accomplish the goal. Individual rights are set aside because the whole is much more important than the part. Time flies, morale soars upward, heroic stories are told, and commitment is the watchword. Why? Because the leader has a vision!

All that is necessary to remove the excitement from the preceding paragraph is one word—*vision*. Without it, energy ebbs low, deadlines are missed, personal agendas begin to surface, production falls, and people scatter.

Helen Keller was asked, "What would be worse than being born blind?" She replied, "To have sight without vision." Sadly, too many people are placed into leadership positions without a vision for the organization that they will lead. All great leaders possess two things: They know where they are going, and they are able to persuade others to follow. They are like the sign in an optometrist's office: "If you don't see what you want, you've come to the right place." This chapter will deal with the leader's foresight and the ability to gather people around it.

The word *vision* has perhaps been overused in the last few years. The first goal of many a management workshop is to develop a statement of purpose for the organization. Others will look at you oddly if you cannot recite your organization's purpose by memory and produce a card with the statement of purpose printed on it.

Why all the pressure to develop a purpose for your organization? There are two reasons. First, vision becomes the distinctive, rallying cry of the organization. It is a clear statement in a competitive market that you have an important niche among all the voices clamoring for customers. It is your real reason for existence. Second, vision becomes the new control tool, replacing the 1,000-page manual that is boxy and constrains initiative. In an age when decentralization all the way to the front line is required to survive, the vision is the key that keeps everyone focused.

VISION STATEMENTS

What you see is what you can be. This deals with your potential. I have often asked myself, does the vision make the leader? Or, does the leader make the vision?

I believe the vision comes first. I have known many leaders who lost the vision and, therefore, lost their power to lead. People do what people see. That is the greatest motivational principle in the world. Stanford Research says that 89 percent of what we learn is visual, 10 percent of what we learn is auditory, and 1 percent of what we learn is through other senses.

In other words, people depend on visual stimulation for growth.

Couple a vision with a leader willing to implement that dream, and a movement begins. People do not follow a dream in itself. They follow the leader who has that dream and the ability to communicate it effectively. Therefore, vision in the beginning will make a leader, but for that vision to grow and demand a following, the leader must take responsibility for it.

FOUR VISION LEVELS OF PEOPLE

1. Some people never see it. (They are wanderers.)

2. Some people see it but never pursue it on their own. (They are followers.)

3. Some people see it and pursue it. (They are achievers.)

4. Some people see it and pursue it and help others see it. (They are leaders.)

Hubert H. Humphrey is an example of "what you see is what you can be." During a trip to Washington, D.C., in 1935, he wrote this in a letter to his wife: "Honey, I see how someday, if you and I just apply ourselves and make up our minds to work for bigger and better things, we can someday live here in Washington and probably be in government, politics, or service . . . Oh, gosh, I hope my dream comes true—I'm going to try anyhow."

> All great leaders possess two things: one, they know where they are going, and two, they are able to persuade others to follow.

YOU SEE WHAT YOU ARE PREPARED TO SEE

This deals with perception. Konrad Adenauer was correct when he said, "We all live under the same sky, but we don't all have the same horizon."

Automobile genius Henry Ford once came up with a revolutionary plan for a new kind of engine. We know it today as the V-8. Ford was eager to get his great new idea into production. He had some men draw up the plans and presented them to the engineers.

As the engineers studied the drawings, one by one they came to the same conclusion. Their visionary boss just didn't know much about the fundamental principles of engineering. He'd have to be told gently—his dream was impossible.

Ford said, "Produce it anyway."

They replied, "But it's impossible."

"Go ahead," Ford commanded, "and stay on the job until you succeed, no matter how much time is required."

For six months they struggled with drawing after drawing, design after design. Nothing. Another six months. Nothing. At the end of the year, Ford checked with his engineers, and once again they told him that what he wanted was impossible. Ford told them to keep going. They did. And they discovered how to build a V-8 engine.

Henry Ford and his engineers both lived under the same sky, but they didn't all have the same horizon.

In *A Savior for All Seasons*, William Barker related the story of a bishop from the East Coast who many years ago paid a visit to a small, Midwestern religious college. He stayed at the home of the college president, who also served as professor of physics and chemistry. After dinner the bishop declared that the millennium couldn't be far off, because just about everything about nature had been discovered and all inventions conceived.

The young college president politely disagreed and said he felt there would be many more discoveries. When the angered bishop challenged the president to name just one such invention, the president replied he was certain that within fifty years men would be able to fly.

"Nonsense!" sputtered the outraged bishop. "Only angels are intended to fly."

The bishop's name was Wright, and he had two boys at home who

> Leaders can never take their people farther than they have traveled. Like leader, like people.

would prove to have greater vision than their father. Their names were Orville and Wilbur. The father and his sons both lived under the same sky, but they didn't all have the same horizon.

How can this be? Why is it that two people can be in the same place at the same time and both see entirely different things? It's simple. We see what we are prepared to see, not what is. Every successful leader understands this about people and asks three questions: What do others see; why do they see it that way; and how can I change their perception?

WHAT YOU SEE IS WHAT YOU GET

The following illustration originated in Luis Palau's book *Dream Great Dreams* (Multnomah Press, 1984).

Think about how nice and refreshing it is to taste a cold Coke. Hundreds of millions of people around the world have enjoyed this experience, thanks to the vision of Robert Woodruff. During his tenure as president of Coca-Cola (1923–1955), Woodruff boldly declared, "We will see that every man in uniform gets a bottle of Coca-Cola for five cents wherever he is and whatever the costs." When World War II had ended, Woodruff stated that before he died he wanted every person in the world to have tasted Coca-Cola. Robert Woodruff was a man of vision!

With careful planning and a lot of persistence, Woodruff and his colleagues reached their generation around the globe for Coke.

> God's gift to me is my potential. My gift back to God is what I do with that potential.

When Disney World first opened, Mrs. Walt Disney was asked to speak at the Grand Opening, since Walt had died. She was introduced by a man who said, "Mrs. Disney, I just wish Walt could have seen this." She stood up and said, "He did," and sat down. Walt Disney knew it. Robert Woodruff knew it. Even Flip Wilson knew it! What you see is what you get.

At this point, I feel compelled to ask a question before we go on to the subject of personal ownership of a vision: "Is my dream going to make a difference in the world in which I live?"

Bobb Biehl, in his book *Increasing Your Leadership Confidence*, says, "Keep in mind the difference between a winner's and a loser's mentality. Winners focus on winning big—not just how to win, but how to win big. Losers, however, don't focus on losing; they just focus on getting by!"[2]

Keep asking yourself, "Survival, success, or significance?" Are you striving to simply survive, are you dreaming about success, or are you really out to make a truly significant difference?

Moishe Rosen teaches a one-sentence mental exercise that's an effective tool in dreaming. It is simply this:

If I had _____,

I would _____.

If you had anything you wanted—unlimited time, unlimited money, unlimited information, unlimited staff—all the resources you could ask for, what would you do? Your answer to that question is your dream. Make it worthwhile.

One day Lucy and Linus had a chicken wishbone and were going to pull it to make a wish. Lucy explained to Linus that if he got the bigger half of the wishbone, his wish would come true. Linus said, "Do I have to say the wish out loud?" Lucy said, "Of course. If you don't say it out loud, it won't come true." So Lucy went ahead and made her wish first. She said, "I wish for four new sweaters, a new bike, a new pair of skates, a new dress, and one hundred dollars." Then it was time for Linus to make his wish. He said, "I wish for a long life for all my friends, I wish for world peace, I wish for great advancements in medical research." About that time, Lucy took the wishbone and threw it away. She said, "Linus, that's the trouble with you. You're always spoiling everything."

PERSONAL OWNERSHIP OF A VISION

My friend Rick Warren says, "If you want to know the temperature of your organization, put a thermometer in the leader's mouth." Leaders can never take their people farther than they have traveled. Therefore, the focus of vision must be on the leader—like leader, like people. Followers find the leader and then the vision. Leaders find the vision and then the people.

I am asked many questions when I speak at leadership conferences throughout the country. One of the most common questions asked by those in leadership positions is: "How do I get a vision for my organization?" This question is crucial. Until it is answered, a person will be a leader in name only. Although I cannot give you a vision, I can share the process of receiving one for you and those around you.

LOOK WITHIN YOU: WHAT DO YOU FEEL?

Theodore Hesburgh said, "The very essence of leadership is that you have a vision. It's got to be a vision you can articulate clearly and forcefully on every occasion. You can't blow an uncertain trumpet." An "uncertain trumpet" is usually the result of an individual who either lacks a vision or is trying to lead with someone else's dream. Certain trumpet sounds come forth from a leader who has birthed a vision from within. There is a vast difference between a person with a vision and a visionary person.

- A person with a vision talks little but does much.

- A visionary person does little but talks much.

- A person with a vision finds strength from inner convictions.

- A visionary person finds strength from outward conditions.

- A person with vision continues when problems arise.

- A visionary person quits when the road becomes difficult.

Many great people began life in the poorest and most humble of homes, with little education and no advantages. Thomas Edison was a newsboy on trains. Andrew Carnegie started work at $4 a month, John D. Rockefeller at $6 a week. The remarkable thing about Abraham Lincoln was not that he was born in a log cabin, but that he got out of the log cabin.

Demosthenes, the greatest orator of the ancient world, stuttered! The first time he tried to make a public speech, he was laughed off the rostrum. Julius Caesar was an epileptic. Napoleon was of humble parentage and far from being a born genius (he stood forty-sixth in his class at the military academy in a class of sixty-five). Beethoven was deaf, as was Thomas Edison. Charles Dickens was lame; so was Handel. Homer was blind; Plato was a hunchback; Sir Walter Scott was paralyzed.

What gave these great individuals the stamina to overcome severe setbacks and become successful? Each person had an inner dream that lit a fire that could not be extinguished. Great visions begin as an "inside job." Napoleon Hill said, "Cherish your visions and dreams as they are the children of your soul: the blueprints of your ultimate achievements."

LOOK BEHIND YOU: WHAT HAVE YOU LEARNED?

A person without experience sees a vision idealistically. To this individual the vision alone is enough. Naively this person casts the vision to others, expecting the dream to do the work and failing to realize that a vision needs support. A person with experience learns that people buy into the leader *before* they buy into the vision. Experienced leaders realize that people are fickle and dreams are fragile. Experience has taught me these principles about vision:

- The credibility of a vision is determined by the leader.
- The acceptance of a vision is determined by the timing of its presentation.
- The value of a vision is determined by the energy and direction it gives.
- The evaluation of a vision is determined by the commitment level of people.

- The success of a vision is determined by its ownership by both the leader and the people.

Leonard Lauder, president of Estee Lauder, said, "When a person with experience meets a person with money, the person with experience will get the money. And the person with the money will get the experience."

LOOK AROUND YOU: WHAT IS HAPPENING TO OTHERS?

A little boy attended his first symphonic concert. He was excited by the splendid hall, the beautiful people in their formal finery, and the sound of the large, enthusiastic orchestra. Of all the instruments in the orchestra, however, his favorite was the cymbals. The first loud, dramatic crash of those brass disks won him over without reservation. He noticed, though, that most of the evening the cymbal player stood motionless while the other musicians played. Only occasionally was the cymbal player called upon to make his contribution, and even then his time of glory was quite brief.

After the concert, the little boy's parents took him backstage to meet some of the musicians. The little fellow immediately sought out the cymbalist. "Say, mister," he said sincerely, "how much do you need to know to play the cymbals?" The musician laughed and answered, "You don't have to know much at all. You only have to know when."

A good idea becomes great when the people are ready. The individual who is impatient with people will be defective in leadership. The evidence of strength lies not in streaking ahead, but in adapting your stride to the slower pace of others while not forfeiting your lead. If we run too far ahead, we lose our power to influence.

LOOK AHEAD OF YOU: WHAT IS THE BIG PICTURE?

This question often separates leaders from managers. Leaders are concerned with the organization's basic purpose—why it exists and what it should achieve. They are not preoccupied with the "how to" or nuts-and-bolts aspect of the operation.

LOOK ABOVE YOU: WHAT DOES GOD EXPECT OF YOU?

Richard E. Day said, "Every golden era in human history proceeds from the devotion and righteous passion of some single individual. There are no bona fide mass movements; it just looks that way. There is always one man who knows his God and knows where he is going."

God's gift to me is my potential. My gift back to God is what I do with that potential. I believe great leaders sense a "higher calling"— one that lifts them above themselves. What a terrible waste of life to be climbing the ladder of success only to find when you reach the top that you were leaning against the wrong building. Great visions are bigger than the person. My definition of success is:

knowing God and His desires for me;
growing to my maximum potential; and
sowing seeds that benefit others.

LOOK BESIDE YOU: WHAT RESOURCES ARE AVAILABLE TO YOU?

A vision should be greater than the person who has it. Its accomplishment must be the result of many people bringing many resources to the job. Many times I have read the speech of President John F. Kennedy that cast the vision of America landing on the moon during the decade of the '60s. That dream captured the people and resources of our country and became a reality.

The experienced leader is always looking for others to make the dream come true. My top priority in the vision for the twenty-five-million-dollar relocation of the congregation I pastor is to develop and find winners to help make the vision a reality. I continually evaluate the progress of this relocation project by the commitment of the people.

Too often leaders hesitate to test the commitment levels of those around them. What is the result? They are never sure where the project stands, or where their people stand. I remember well the conclusions I felt when we finished our first four-million-dollar fund-raising effort. We worked hard, and I knew where the people stood.

The leader continually passes on the vision to those who come around, knowing that dreams, if presented right, are contagious.

In the movie *Tucker: The Man and His Dream*, Abe, the bottom-line businessman and beleaguered bookkeeper for Preston Tucker, who conceived a radical new automobile—a low-cost car with fuel injector, rear-mounted engine, disc brakes, pop-out windows, seat belts, and aerodynamic design—caught Tucker's dream.

Despite a misremembered warning from his mother, he bought a share of Tucker's idealism.

Abe thought his mother said, "Don't get too close to people; you'll catch their dreams."

Years later he realized she had said *germs*, not *dreams*.[3]

CORPORATE OWNERSHIP OF A VISION

A vision is a clear picture of what the leader sees his or her group being or doing. According to a survey reported by *Leadership* magazine, communicating a vision is one of the most frustrating areas of leading an organization.

Recently I was a guest on a radio talk show. The host poured out his frustration to me during the break concerning this very issue. He said, "I have a vision for my people but find it difficult to transfer that vision to others." One fact is true: leaders who effectively communicate goals to their followers achieve far more than those who don't.

Successful leaders see on three levels:

Level 1. Perception: seeing what is now with the eyes of reality
Level 2. Probability: seeing what will be with the eyes of discernment
Level 3. Possibility: seeing what can be with the eyes of vision

A *futurist* lives only on Level 3. A *forecaster* lives only on Level 2. A *follower* lives only on Level 1. A *leader* lives on Level 3, leads on Level 2, and listens on Level 1.

For example, an organization sets changing its name as a goal. The great leader, through eyes of vision, already sees a new name for the company (Level 3). That leader, through the eyes of discernment, sees the trend of the organization (Level 2). The leader knows the direction of the company by looking through the eyes of reality (Level 1).

Surprisingly, vision casting does not begin with Level 3 (the big picture). It begins with Level 1 (the small picture) and will only be successful if the leader can influence Level 2 (the next picture).

Understanding What Hinders a Vision—Level 1

We see things, not as they are, but as we are. Therefore, when a vision is hindered, it is usually a people problem. There are ten types of people who usually hinder the vision of the organization.

1. Limited Leaders

Everything rises and falls on leadership. That statement is certainly true with vision casting. A limited leader will either lack the vision or the ability to successfully pass it on.

The prime minister of France once said, "If you are doing big things, you attract big men. If you are doing little things, you attract little men. Little men usually cause trouble." Then he paused, shook his head sadly, and added, "We are having an awful lot of trouble.

2. Concrete Thinkers

George Bernard Shaw said, "Some men see things as they are and say, 'Why?' [concrete thinker] I dream of things that never were and say 'Why not?' [creative thinker]"

Charlie Brown holds up his hands before his friend Lucy and says,

"These are hands which may someday accomplish great things. These are hands which may someday do marvelous works! They may build mighty bridges, or heal the sick, or hit home runs, or write soul-stirring novels! These are hands which may someday change the course of destiny!"

Lucy, who always sees things as they are, replies, "They've got jelly on them."

3. Dogmatic Talkers

Many visions aren't realized because of strong, dogmatic people. To be absolutely certain about something, one must either know everything or nothing about it. Most of the time, the dogmatist knows nothing but conventionally says something. For example, "Everything that can be invented has been invented." That was Charles H. Duell, director of the U.S. Patent Office, speaking in 1899! Of course, Duell was not alone. President Grover Cleveland once commented (in 1905) that "sensible and responsible women do not want to vote." Then there was Robert Miliken, Nobel Prize winner in physics, who said in 1923, "There is no likelihood man can ever tap the power of the atom." Lord Kelvin, president of England's Royal Society (a scientific organization), noted in 1885, "Heavier-than-air flying machines are impossible."

My favorite is a statement of baseball great Tris Speaker. He was quoted in 1921 as saying, "[Babe] Ruth made a big mistake when he gave up pitching."

4. Continual Losers

Many people look at their past failures and fear the risk of pursuing a vision. Their motto is, "If at first you don't succeed, destroy all evidence that you've tried." They also destroy everyone's attempt to ever try again.

5. Satisfied Sitters

People strive for comfort, predictability, and security in life. On the heels of comfort comes complacency; of predictability, boredom; and of security, a lack of vision. A nest is good for a robin while it is an egg. But it is bad for a robin when it has wings. It's a good place to be hatched in, but it's a poor place to fly in. It's always sad when people don't want to leave the nests of their lives.

In a *Leadership* magazine article, Lynn Anderson described what happens when people lose their vision. A group of pilgrims landed on the shores of America nearly four hundred years ago. With great vision and courage they had come to settle in the new land. In the first year, they established a town. In the second, they elected town council. In the third, the government proposed building a road five miles westward into the wilderness. But in the fourth year, the people tried to impeach the town council because the people thought such a road into the forest was a waste of public funds. Somehow these forward-looking people had lost their vision. Once able to see across oceans, they now could not look five miles into the wilderness.

6. Tradition Lovers

The British have always been good with the patronage system. John F. Barker in *Roll Call* tells the story that for more than twenty years, for no apparent reason, an attendant stood at the foot of the stairway leading to the House of Commons. At last someone checked and discovered that the job had been held in the attendant's family for three generations. It seems it originated when the stairs were painted and the current attendant's grandfather was assigned the task of warning people not to step on the wet paint.

One British newsman, told of the situation, commented, "The paint dried up but not the job."

7. Census Takers

Some people never feel comfortable stepping out of the crowd. They desire to be a part of, not apart from, the group. These people will only embrace the vision when the majority does. They are never in front.

True leaders are always in the minority because they are thinking ahead of the present majority. Even when the majority catches up, these leaders will have moved ahead and so, again, will be in the minority.[4]

8. Problem Perceivers

Some people can see a problem in every solution. Usually obstacles are the things you see when you take your eyes off the goal. Interestingly, some people think the ability to see problems is a mark of maturity. Not so. It's the mark of a person without a vision. These people abort great visions by presenting problems without any solutions.

Cardinal John Henry Newman said that nothing would get done at all if a man waited until he could do something so well that no one could find fault with it.

9. Self-Seekers

People who live for themselves are in a mighty small business. They also never accomplish much. Great goals are only reached by the united effort of many. Selfish people are vision busters.

10. Failure Forecasters

Some people have a faculty for touching the wrong keys. From the finest instrument, they extract only discord. All their songs are in a minor key. They send the note of pessimism everywhere. The shadows dominate all their pictures. Their outlook is always gloomy, times are always bad, and money is tight. Everything in them seems to be contracting; nothing in their lives expands or grows.

These people are like the man who gathered with many others at the Hudson River to see the first steamship launched. He kept saying, "They'll never get her going. They'll never get her going." But they did. The steamship belched and moved out fast. Immediately the same man said, "They'll never get her stopped. They'll never get her stopped."

I love the Chinese proverb that states, "Man who says, 'It cannot be done' should not interrupt man who is doing it."

SETTING THE PROPER ENVIRONMENT—LEVEL 2

Knowing people and the keys to their lives will allow the leader to go to the "next picture" in Level 2. It is essential that the leader begin to influence what will be seen by the people. Remember, if the leader and a few others see Level 3, then only they will know if Level 2 is set correctly to take others into the vision area. The following steps will set Level 2 correctly.

COME ALONGSIDE OF THEM

Let them see your heart before they see your hope. People don't care how much you see until they see how much you care. I emphasize again: people buy into the leader before they buy into that leader's vision. Cultivate trust. Be transparent and patient. Start where they are by seeing through their eyes. Seek to find their hopes and dreams. Begin building a bridge between the vision of the organization and their personal goals. Done correctly, both can be accomplished. Go for the win-win. Remember, when you help people get what they want, they will help you get what you want. This can only be accomplished by building strong relationships with people.

PAINT THE PICTURE FOR THEM

One time I read that a great teacher never strives to explain his vision; he simply invites you to stand beside him and see for yourself. I agree with the relationship part of this statement, but I believe great leaders explain their vision by painting a picture for the people. John W. Patterson, founder of National Cash Register, said, "I have been trying all my life, first to see for myself, and then to get other people to see with me. To succeed in business it is necessary to make the other man see things as you see them. Seeing . . . was the objective. In the broadest sense, I am a visualizer."

Every great vision has certain ingredients, and the great leader makes the people understand, appreciate, and "see" them:

Horizon: A leader's vision of the horizon allows people to see the heights of their possibilities. Each individual will determine how high he or she wants to go. Your responsibility is to put plenty of sky into the picture. Paul Harvey said that a blind man's world is bounded by the limits of his touch; an ignorant man's world by the limits of his knowledge; a great man's world by the limits of his vision.

Sun: This element represents warmth and hope. Light brings out the optimism in people. A prime function of a leader is to keep hope alive. Napoleon said, "Leaders are dealers in hope."

Mountains: Every vision has its challenges. Edwin Land, founder of Polaroid, said, "The first thing you do is teach the person to feel that the vision is very important and nearly impossible. That draws out the drive in the winner."

Birds: This element represents freedom and the spirit of man. Watching an eagle rise causes you to feel your own spirit soar. "Wars may be fought with weapons, but it is the spirit of the men who fight and of the man who leads that gains victory."[5]

Flowers: The journey toward the realization of any great vision takes time. Make sure the scenery includes rest stops—places to smell flowers and become refreshed mentally and physically. Success is the progressive realization of a predetermined, worthwhile goal.

Path: People need direction, a place to begin, and a path to follow. A traveler through a rugged country asked his Indian guide, "How are you able to pick your way over these jagged peaks, by treacherous trails, without ever losing your direction?"

The guide answered, "I have the near look and the far vision. With the one I see what is directly ahead of me; with the other I guide my course by the stars."[6]

Yourself: Never paint the vision without placing yourself in the picture. This will show your commitment to the vision and your desire to walk with the people through the process. They need a model to follow. As Warren R. Austin said in *UN World*, "If you would lift me, you must be on higher ground."

Why should a leader paint the picture and place these essentials in it? Roger von Oech, in his book, *A Kick in the Seat of the Pants*, gives an excellent answer:

> Take a look around where you're sitting and find five things that have blue in them. Go ahead and do it.
>
> With a "blue" mind-set, you'll find that blue jumps out at you: a blue book on the table, a blue pillow on the couch, blue in the painting on the wall, and so on.
>
> In like fashion, you've probably noticed that after you buy a new car, you promptly see that make of car everywhere. That's because people find what they are looking for.[7]

The leader helps the people develop this sensitivity and an eye for knowing what to look for. If the picture is painted clearly and shown continually, soon others will begin to see how to see how it fits into everything they do. They will have a vision mind-set. Then there will be only one thing left to bring the vision into the ownership of others.

PUT THE THINGS THEY LOVE IN THE PICTURE

People carry pictures of other people and things they love. Put what is important to the people within the frame of the vision and you will have transferred the vision to the people.

During World War II, parachutes were being constructed by the thousands. From the workers' point of view, the job was tedious. It involved crouching over a sewing machine eight to ten hours a day and stitching endless lengths of colorless fabric. The result was a formless heap of cloth. But every morning the workers were told that each stitch was part of a life-saving operation. They were asked to think as they sewed that each para-chute might be the one worn by their husbands, their brothers, their sons.

Although the work was hard and the hours long, the women and the men on the home front understood their contribution to the larger picture.[8]

Opening Eyes to Possibilities—Level 3

On this level we need to ask ourselves how to grow people to the size of the vision. This represents the one thing the leader must continually do . . . grow people to the vision once they see it.

There are several steps a Level 3 leader must take. First, the leader must seek and find winners to add to the team. These qualities of win-ners will guide the search:

- Winners are less sensitive to disapproval and rejection—they brush it off.
- Winners think "bottom line."
- Winners focus on the task at hand.
- Winners are not superstitious—they say, "That's life."
- Winners refuse to equate failure with self-worth.
- Winners don't restrict thinking to established, rigid patterns.
- Winners see the big picture.
- Winners welcome challenge with optimism.
- Winners don't waste time in unproductive thought.

Once the winners are added to the team, they join others as the major influencers in the organization. At this point, it is extremely important for the leader to spend time with the influencers to discover the "keys" to their lives. What is most valued by these influencers should help them through tough personal issues; provide a time and place for them to grow; add value to their family and job; assist them in finding their strengths; and plug them into the organization.

Also, it is very important for the leader to mentor these winners. They should be exposed to great books (past and present), great places, great events, and great people. They should find great ideas in you, the leader, and they should develop a desire to pursue your interests and vision in an attempt to build a mutually beneficial relationship. When this occurs, you will find that the winners naturally pass on the vision that you hold dear for your organization and for them.

The successful Level 3 leader will see on three levels:

1. *The Perceptible Level:* What is now seen—the eyes of reality. A leader listens on this level.

2. *The Probable Level:* What will be seen—the eyes of discernment. A leader leads on this level.

3. *The Possible Level:* What can be seen—the eyes of vision. A leader lives on this level.

Vision is empowering to the leader who has it. The leader with vision believes not only that what he envisions can be done, but that it must be done. There was a study done of concentration camp survivors regarding the common characteristics of those who did not succumb in the concentration camps. Viktor Frankl was a living answer to that question. He was a successful Viennese psychiatrist before the Nazis threw him into such a camp. Years later, when giving lectures, he would say:

> There is only one reason why I am here today. What kept me alive was you. Others gave up hope. I dreamed that some day I would be here telling you how I, Viktor Frankl, had survived Nazi

concentration camps. I've never been here before, I've never seen any of you before, I've never given this speech before. But in my dreams I have stood before you and said these words a thousand times.

It was the vision that made the difference. As a young man I learned this poem. It is an appropriate way to end this chapter.

> Ah, great it is to believe the dream,
> As we stand in youth by the starry stream.
> But a greater thing is to live life through,
> And say at the end, the dream came true.

Leaders do that for themselves, and others.

NINE

THE PRICE TAG OF LEADERSHIP:
SELF-DISCIPLINE

I n reading the lives of great men, I found that the first victory they won was over themselves . . . Self-discipline with all of them came first."[1]

The Greek word for *self-control* comes from a root word meaning "to grip" or "take hold of." This word describes people who are willing to get a grip on their lives and take control of areas that will bring them success or failure.

Aristotle used this same word to describe "the ability to test desire by reason . . . to be resolute and ever in readiness to end natural vent and pain." He explained that people who are not controlled have strong desires which try to seduce them from the way of reason; but to succeed they must keep those desires under control.

Once, while conducting a leadership seminar, I defined discipline in the beginning of life as the choice of achieving what you really want by doing things you don't really want to do. After successfully doing this for some time, discipline becomes the choice of achieving what you really want by doing things you now want to do! I truly believe we can become disciplined and enjoy it—after years of practicing it.

All great leaders have understood that their number one responsibility was for their own discipline and personal growth. If they could not lead themselves, they could not lead others. Leaders can never take others farther than they have gone themselves, for no one can travel without until he or she has first traveled within. A great person will lead a great organization, but growth is only possible when the leader is willing to "pay the price" for it. Many potentially gifted leaders have stopped short of the payment line and found out that shortcuts don't pay off in the long run.

This is what Edwin Markham has to say about human worth:

> We are blind until we see
> That in the human plan
> Nothing is worth the making
> If it does not make the man.
> Why build these cities glorious
> If man unbuilded goes?
> In vain we build the world
> Unless the builder also grows.[2]

THE PROCESS FOR DEVELOPING PERSONAL DISCIPLINE

Frederick the Great of Prussia was walking on the outskirts of Berlin when he encountered a very old man proceeding in the opposite direction.

"Who are you?" asked Frederick.

"I am a king," replied the old man.

"A king!" laughed Frederick. "Over what kingdom do you reign?"

"Over myself," was the proud reply.

"Reigning" over yourself requires personal discipline.

START WITH YOURSELF

A reporter once asked the great evangelist D. L. Moody which people gave him the most trouble. He answered immediately, "I've had more trouble with D. L. Moody than any man alive." The late Samuel

Hoffenstein said, "Wherever I go, I go too, and spoil everything." And there is the classic Jack Paar line, "Looking back, my life seems to be one long obstacle course, with me as the chief obstacle."

> We cannot travel without until we first travel within.

My observation is that more potential leaders fail because of inner issues than outer ones.

Each month I teach a leadership lesson to my staff, which is recorded live and sent to other leaders across the United States. Recently I spoke on the subject "How to Get out of Your Own Way." A tremendous response was received from many listeners, who said, "The lesson was needed in my life. I am my worst problem!" Most of us can relate to the sign I

> When we are foolish, we want to conquer the world. When we are wise, we want to conquer ourselves.

saw in an office: "If you could kick the person responsible for most of your troubles, you wouldn't be able to sit down for weeks."

Your Competitor

An enemy I had, whose face I stoutly strove to know,
For hard he dogged my steps unseen, wherever I did go.
My plans he balked, my aims he foiled, he blocked my onward way.
When for some lofty goal I toiled, he grimly said to me, Nay.
One night I seized him and held him fast, from him the veil did draw,
I looked upon his face at last and lo . . . myself I saw.

When we are foolish, we want to conquer the world. When we are wise, we want to conquer ourselves.

START EARLY

Perhaps the most valuable result of all education is the ability to make yourself do the thing you have to do, when it ought to be done, whether you like it or not; it is the first lesson that ought to be learned and, however early a man's training begins, it is probably the last lesson that he learns thoroughly.

My parents modeled discipline and insisted that their three children develop that lifestyle. Time management, hard work, persistence, honesty, responsibility, and a positive attitude, regardless of the situation, were always expected of us. However, I didn't appreciate this training until I went to college. There I saw many students who couldn't get a grip on their lives or their studies. I began to realize that I had a decided advantage over others because of the disciplines already "under my belt." It is true—when you do the things you ought to do when you ought to do them, the day will come when you will do the things you want to do when you want to do them. Hard work is the accumulation of the easy things you didn't do when you should have.

> Hard work is the accumulation of easy things you didn't do when you should have.

> What you are going to be tomorrow, you are becoming today.

START SMALL

What you are going to be tomorrow, you are becoming today. It is essential to begin developing self-discipline in a small way today in order to be disciplined in a big way tomorrow.

A Small Plan That Will Make a Big Difference

1. List five areas in your life that lack discipline.

2. Place them in order of your priority for conquering them.

3. Take them on, one at a time.

4. Secure resources, such as books and tapes, that will give you instruction and motivation to conquer each area.

5. Ask a person who models the trait you want to possess to hold you accountable for it.

6. Spend fifteen minutes each morning getting focused in order to get control of this weak area in your life.

7. Do a five-minute checkup on yourself at midday.

8. Take five minutes in the evening to evaluate your progress.

9. Allow sixty days to work on one area before you go to the next.

10. Celebrate with the one who holds you accountable as you show continued success.

Remember, having it all doesn't mean having it all at once. It takes time. Start small and concentrate on today. The slow accumulation of disciplines will one day make a big difference. Ben Franklin said, "It is easier to suppress the first desire than to satisfy all that follow it."

START NOW

As John Hancock Field says, "All worthwhile men have good thoughts, good ideas, and good intentions, but precious few of them ever translate those into action."

In 1976, Indiana University's basketball team was undefeated throughout the regular season and captured the NCAA National Championship. Controversial and colorful coach Bobby Knight led them to that championship. Shortly afterward, Coach Knight was interviewed on the

> Great leaders never set themselves above their followers except in carrying out responsibilities.

television show *60 Minutes*. The commentators asked him, "Why is it, Bobby, that your basketball teams at Indiana are always so successful? Is it the will to succeed?"

"The will to succeed is important," Knight replied, "but I'll tell you what's more important: It's the will to prepare. It's the will to go out there every day training and building those muscles and sharpening those skills!"

> Success depends not merely on how well you do the things you enjoy, but how conscientiously you perform those duties you don't.

Abraham Lincoln said, "I will get ready, and then perhaps my chance will come." Too often the disciplines have not been developed and an opportunity is missed. Charlie Brown of the *Peanuts* comic strip once said that his life was mixed up because he missed all of the rehearsals. Before you can become a "star," you have to start. Now is the best time.

ORGANIZE YOUR LIFE

"One of the advantages of being disorderly is that one is constantly making exciting discoveries." That statement by A. A. Milne is true, but the discoveries are usually too late and consequently an opportunity is missed. Then you as a leader are perceived as being "out of control." This leads to uncertainty and insecurity among followers.

When you are organized, you have a special power. You walk with a sure sense of purpose. Your priorities are clear in your mind. You orchestrate complex events with a masterful touch. Things fall into place when you reveal your plans. You move smoothly from one project to the next with no wasted motion. Throughout the day you gain stamina and momentum as your successes build. People believe your promises because you always follow through. When you enter a meeting, you are prepared for whatever they throw at you. When at last you show your hand, you're a winner.

Christopher Robin, in *Winnie the Pooh*, gives my favorite definition of organization: "Organizing is what you do before you do something, so that when you do it, it's not all mixed up."

Here is my top ten list for personal organization:

1. SET YOUR PRIORITIES

Two things are difficult to get people to do. The first is to do things in order of importance, and the second is to *continue* doing things in order of importance. William Gladstone said, "He is a wise man who wastes no energy on pursuits for which he is not fitted; and he is wiser still who from among the things he can do well, chooses and resolutely follows the best."

Major events in my life, such as my speaking at conferences, are scheduled a year or two in advance. The last week of each month I spend two hours planning my schedule for the next thirty days. On paper I list all my major responsibilities according to importance and time needed to accomplish those tasks. This becomes the gauge to help me "keep on track" and keep moving. As each assignment is completed in its allotted time, I check it off my monthly list.

2. PLACE YOUR PRIORITIES IN YOUR CALENDAR

Once this list is written out on paper, I give it to my personal assistant, who writes it on my calendar. This protects me from outside pressures that clamor daily for my time. This also makes me accountable to someone else who can help me stay on track.

3. ALLOW A LITTLE TIME FOR THE UNEXPECTED

The kinds of work you do will determine the amount of time you set aside for interruptions. For example, the more you interact with people, the more time you must set aside. I set aside one-half day each week in my calendar for the unexpected.

4. DO PROJECTS ONE AT A TIME

A good general fights only on one front at a time. That is also true of a good leader. A feeling of being overwhelmed is the result of too many projects clamoring for your attention. For years I have followed this simple process:

> Itemize all that needs to be done.
> Prioritize things in order of importance.
> Organize each project.
> Emphasize only one project at a time.

5. ORGANIZE YOUR WORK SPACE

My work space is organized in two places: administrative and creative. My administrative office includes a room for small-group meetings, my work desk, and a desk for my personal assistant. This allows me to constantly communicate any details immediately to my key people. This office contains my calendar, computers, and files, and allows me easy access to administrative help. My creative office is separated from everyone. It contains my books, a copy machine, and my writing files. This secluded place is off-limits to my staff and allows me a proper environment for thinking, reading, and writing.

6. WORK ACCORDING TO YOUR TEMPERAMENT

If you are a morning person, organize your most important work for the morning hours. Obviously, if you are a late starter, do the opposite. However, be sure not to allow the weaknesses of your temperament to excuse you from what you know you need to do to work most effectively.

7. USE YOUR DRIVING TIME FOR LIGHT WORK AND GROWTH

My father gave me some great advice the day I became sixteen and received my driver's license. Climbing into the passenger side of the car, he placed a book in my glove compartment and said, "Son, never be in a car without a book. Whenever you are delayed in traffic, you can pull out this book and read." My car also contains many tapes for me to listen to and a notepad to jot down thoughts. My hands-free car phone also allows me to make calls to people on the way home from work. Recently while driving, I made twenty-one calls and saved hours of office time. Many times I take a staff person with me so we can discuss business and develop a closer relationship. I estimate that the average person could achieve eight additional hours of personal growth and work in each week by using driving time wisely.

8. Develop Systems That Work for You

Bobb Biehl says, "Systems—from to-do lists and calendars to libraries and computers—are your servants. They help you do things better and quicker, and by improving them, you decrease your time expenses and increase your results." Don't fight systems. Improve them.

9. Always Have a Plan for Those Minutes Between Meetings

Hours can be saved by making the best use of minutes. I keep a list of things to do that can be done anywhere in very short amounts of time. There are calls to make, memos to reply to or send, reports to scan, thank-you notes to write, and communications to share. Keep handy a list of things you can do in a short time.

10. Focus on Results, Not the Activity

Remember Peter Drucker's definition of efficiency (doing things right) versus effectiveness (doing the right things)? As you spend time on personal organization, be sure to keep your focus on doing the right things, that is, doing what is truly important. Then use this rule of thumb for organizing your overall work strategy:

> Work where you are the strongest 80 percent of the time.
> Work where you are learning 15 percent of the time.
> Work where you are weak 5 percent of the time.

WELCOME RESPONSIBILITY

Winston Churchill said, "The price of greatness is responsibility." To increase your ability to take responsibility, do the following:

Be responsible for who you are. I believe in this. In fact, I'd like you to consider how it relates to research done by a psychologist who studied some people on the bottom.

The psychologist visited a prison and asked various inmates, "Why are you here?" The answers were very revealing, even though expected. There were many of them: "I was framed"; "They ganged up on me"; "It was a case of mistaken identity"; "It was not me—it was somebody else." The psychologist wondered if one could possibly find a larger group of "innocent" people anywhere else but in prison!

That reminds me of one of Abraham Lincoln's favorite stories about the man who murdered both his parents and then, when his sentence was about to be pronounced, pleaded for mercy on the grounds that he was an orphan! As the politician said to the judge, "It's not my fault, Your Honor, I never could have done all that stuff if the people hadn't elected me!"

Be responsible for what you do. It is rare to find a person who will be responsible, who will follow through correctly and finish the job. But when half-finished assignments keep returning to your desk to check up on, verify, edit, and upgrade, obviously someone is failing to take hold of the reins of responsibility.

> I am only one,
> But still I am one.
> I cannot do everything,
> But still I can do something;
> And because I cannot do everything
> I will not refuse to do the
> something that I can do.[3]

Pontius' Puddle

Be responsible for what you have received. John D. Rockefeller Jr. said, "I believe that every right implies a responsibility; every opportunity, an obligation; every possession, a duty." Winston Churchill said, "It is not enough that we do our best; sometimes we have to do what's required." And Jesus said, "Everyone to whom much is given, from him much will be required" (Luke 12:48).

Be responsible to those you lead. Great leaders never set themselves above their followers, except in carrying out responsibilities.

Coach Bo Schembechler tells about the third game of the 1970 season. His University of Michigan Wolverines were playing Texas A&M and they could not move the ball. All of a sudden, Dan Dierdorf, their offensive lineman—who was probably the best in the country at that time—came rushing over to the sidelines. Fed up with the team's performance, he yelled at Schembechler in front of everybody on the sidelines.

"Listen, coach! Run every play over me! Over me! Every play!" And they did. Michigan ran off-tackle six times in a row and marched right down the field. Michigan won the game.

When the game is on the line, great leaders always take responsibility for leading their teams to victory. This is my favorite "take responsibility" story.

The sales manager of a dog-food company asked his salespeople how they liked the company's new advertising program. "Great! Best in the business!" the salespeople responded.

"How do you like our new label and package?"

"Great! Best in the business!" the salespeople responded.

"How do like our sales force?"

They were the sales force. They had to admit they were good. "Okay, then," said the manager. "So we've got the best label, the best package, and the best advertising program being sold by the best sales force in the business. Tell me why we are in seventeenth place in the dog food business."

There was silence. Finally someone said, "It's those lousy dogs. They won't eat the stuff!"

ACCEPT ACCOUNTABILITY

Plato said, "The unexamined life is not worth living." Success and power have often crowded out of the leader's life a willingness to become accountable to others. Leaders in all areas of life are increasingly falling before the public because of this problem. Why does this happen?

HUMAN NATURE CANNOT HANDLE UNCHECKED POWER

Abraham Lincoln said, "Nearly all men can stand adversity, but if you want to test a man's character, give him power." Power can be compared to a great river; while within bounds it is both beautiful and useful. But when it overflows its bounds, it destroys. The danger of power lies in the fact that those who are vested with it tend to make its preservation their first concern. Therefore, they will naturally oppose any changes in the forces that have given them this power. History tells us that power leads to the abuse of power, and abuse of power leads to loss of power.

George Bush prayed in his inaugural address of 1989, "For we are given power not to advance our own purposes nor to make a great show in the world, nor a name. There is but one use of power, and it is to serve people."

LEADERS CAN EASILY BE SEPARATED FROM THEIR PEOPLE

When Harry Truman was thrust into the presidency at the death of FDR, Sam Rayburn gave him some fatherly advice: "From here on out you're going to have lots of people around you. They'll try to put a wall around you and cut you off from any ideas but theirs. They'll tell you what a great man you are, Harry. But you and I both know you ain't."

Hubert H. Humphrey said, "There is no party, no chief executive, no Cabinet, no legislature in this or any other nation, wise enough to govern without constant exposure to informed criticism." That is true for any person who occupies a leadership position.

DEVELOP INTEGRITY

The book *Profiles of Leadership* reveals the answers America's top business and government leaders gave when asked what quality they thought was most important to their success as leaders. Their unanimous answer: *integrity*.

Integrity is the human quality most necessary to business success according to the 1,300 senior executives who responded to a recent survey. Seventy-one percent put it at the top of a list of sixteen traits responsible for enhancing an executive's effectiveness. The dictionary defines integrity as "the state of being complete, unified." When people have integrity, their words and deeds match up. They are who they are, no matter where they are or who they're with. People with integrity are not divided (that's duplicity) or merely pretending (that's hypocrisy). They are "whole," and their lives are "put together." People with integrity have nothing to hide and nothing to fear. Their lives are open books.

Integrity in a leader must be demonstrated daily in a number of tangible ways. These are five that I strive to demonstrate to those I lead.

1. *I will live what I teach.* Deciding what to be is more important than deciding what to do. Often we ask young people "What are you going to do when you grow up?" But the more important question is, "What are you going to *be*?" The character decision must be made before a career is chosen.

Early in my years of leadership, I read this poem by Howard A. Walter and adopted its principles:

Character

I would be true, for there are those who trust me;
I would be pure, for there are those who care;
I would be strong, for there are those who suffer;
I would be brave, for there is much to dare.
I would be friend of all—the foe, the friendless;
I would be giving, and forget the gift;
I would be humble, for I know my weakness;
I would look up, and laugh, and love, and lift.

2. I will do what I say. If I promise something to a subordinate, colleague, or superior, I want to keep my word. The Center for Creative Leadership in Greensboro, North Carolina, released a study of twenty-one high-potential executives who were terminated from their companies or forced to retire early. The one universal character flaw or unforgivable sin which always led to downfall was betraying a trust; that is, not doing something that was promised.

3. I will be honest with others. If those who work with me ever catch me misrepresenting the facts or covering up a problem, I will instantly lose credibility. And it will not be easy to repair.

Dr. William Schultz, a noted psychologist who developed truth-in-management strategies at Proctor and Gamble and NASA, believes the key to productivity is "how well people work together," and he believes that nothing "increases compatibility like mutual trust and honesty." Dr. Schultz says, "If people in business just told the truth, 80 percent to 90 percent of their problems would disappear." Trust and honesty are the means that allow individuals to cooperate so that they can all prosper.

4. I will put what is best for others ahead of what is best for me. The organization I lead and those I work with must come first. When I put the organization's best interests ahead of mine, I keep integrity with those who hired me. When I put the interest of those I work with ahead of mine, I develop friendships and loyalty. Below is the leadership pyramid that I have always tried to follow.

The higher a person rises in an organization, the less personal options and rights they should possess.

5. I will be transparent and vulnerable. Long ago I realized that in working with people, I have two choices. I can close my arms or I can open them. Both choices have strengths and weaknesses. If I close my arms, I won't get hurt, but I will not get much help either. If I open my arms, I likely will get hurt, but I will also receive help. What has been my decision? I've opened my arms and allowed others to enjoy the journey with me. My greatest gift to others is not a job, but myself. That is true of any leader.

PAY NOW, PLAY LATER

There are two paths that people can take. They can either play now and pay later, or pay now and play later. Regardless of the choice, one thing is certain. Life will demand a payment.

My father taught me this important discipline. Each week he would lay out the chores for the next seven days. Many of them could be done anytime during the week. Our goal was to complete them by Saturday noon. If completed, we could do something fun with the family. If not completed, fun was forfeited and that individual stayed home to complete the chore. I needed to miss my deadline only a couple of times to realize that I needed to "pay up front" and finish my work on time.

This lesson has been valuable to me, and I'm teaching it to my children, Elizabeth and Joel Porter. I want them to realize that there is no such thing as a "free lunch," that life is not a gift—it is an investment. The sooner they can take control of their desires and submit them to life's demands, the more successful they will become. John Foster said, "A man without decision of character can never be said to belong to himself. He belongs to whatever can make captive of him." My friend Bill Klassen often reminds me that "when we pay later, the price is greater!"

"I've never known a man worth his salt who in the long run, deep down in his heart, didn't appreciate the grind, the discipline," said Vince Lombardi. "I firmly believe that any man's finest hour—this greatest fulfillment to all he holds dear—is that moment when he has worked his heart out in a good cause and lies exhausted on the field of battle—victorious."

Become Character Driven Instead of Emotion Driven

Most of the significant things done in the world were done by persons who were either too busy or too sick! "There are few ideal and leisurely settings for the disciplines of growth," Robert Thornton Henderson said. "Ninety percent of the work is done in this country by people who don't feel well."

It is not doing the things we like to do, but doing the things we have to do that causes growth and makes us successful. John Luther said, "There's no such thing as a perfect job. In any position you'll find some duties which, if they aren't onerous immediately, eventually will be." Success depends not merely on how well you do the things you enjoy, but how conscientiously you perform those duties you don't.

Tenor Luciano Pavarotti is such a winner. He is often described by his admirers as "the new Caruso." In a newspaper interview, the six-foot, three-hundred-pound tenor asked: "Do you want to know the hardest thing about being a singer? It is to sacrifice yourself every moment of your life, with not one exclusion. For example, if it is raining, don't go out; eat this, do this, sleep ten hours a day. It is not a very free life. You cannot jump on a horse. You cannot go to swim."

Successful people are willing to do things unsuccessful people will not do. My observation is that one of those things that makes a difference is this issue of being character driven instead of emotion driven. This is the difference:

CHARACTER-DRIVEN PEOPLE:	EMOTION-DRIVEN PEOPLE:
do right, then feel good	feel good, then do right
are commitment driven	are convenience driven
make principle-based decisions	make popular based decisions
let action control attitude	let attitude control action
believe it, then see it	see it, then believe it
create momentum	wait for momentum
ask, "What are my responsibilities?"	ask, "What are my rights?"
continue when problems arise	quit when problems arise
are steady	are moody
are leaders	are followers

The late Louis L'Amour is one of the best-selling authors of all time. Nearly 230 million copies of his books are in print worldwide, and every one of his more than one hundred books is still in print. When asked the key to his writing style, he responded, "Start writing, no matter what. The water does not flow until the faucet is turned on."

That's a good word for life. Sometimes, what we need to do is just to do something. Help someone. Sometimes, just getting into action will release power in our lives. We ought to adopt this as our motto for life: "The water does not flow until the faucet is turned on."

Good character is more to be praised than outstanding talent. Most talents are, to some extent, gifts. By contrast, good character is not given to us. We have to build it piece by piece—by thought, choice, courage, and determination. This will only be accomplished with a disciplined lifestyle.

Stephen Covey said:

> If I try to use human influence strategies and tactics of how to get other people to do what I want, to work better, to be more motivated, to like me and each other—while my character is fundamentally flawed, marked by duplicity or insincerity—then, in the long run, I cannot be successful. My duplicity will breed distrust and everything I do even using so-called good human relations techniques will be perceived as manipulative.
>
> It simply makes no difference how good the rhetoric is or even how good the intentions are: if there is little or no trust there is no foundation for permanent success. Only basic goodness gives life to technique.[4]

TEN

THE MOST IMPORTANT LESSON OF LEADERSHIP:

STAFF DEVELOPMENT

The growth and development of people is the highest calling of leadership. Chapter 7 emphasized the general development of people. This chapter will center on the development of a staff, but it is impossible to go into depth on this important subject in one chapter. The intent of this book is to help establish a leadership foundation. Therefore, I have dealt only with basics in the hope that I can help you develop the leader in you. I will write another book that will enable you to develop the leaders around you.

When I turned forty, I began to review my life. I made a list of all the things I was doing at that time. My list included:

senior pastor of a congregation of 3,500 attenders;

oversight and development of thirteen pastors;

president of Injoy, Inc., a company that develops resource materials for thousands of people;

a national and international speaking schedule with over four hundred engagements annually;

producing a monthly leadership tape for Injoy Life Club subscribers;

writing a book every eighteen months;

working on another education degree;

and most important—taking enough time for my wife, Margaret, and our two children, Elizabeth and Joel Porter.

After writing out my list, my conclusion was twofold: I didn't have any more hours, and therefore I couldn't work any harder; and my future growth in production would be determined by my ability to work through other people.

These two realities enabled me to search for and find the most important leadership lesson I've ever learned:

THOSE CLOSEST TO THE LEADER WILL DETERMINE THE LEVEL OF SUCCESS FOR THAT LEADER.

Niccolò Machiavelli said, "The first method for estimating the intelligence of a ruler is to look at the men he has around him." I'm not certain this subject is an issue of IQ, but I am sure that it is a test of leadership. Leaders who continue to grow personally and bring growth to their organizations will influence many and develop a successful team around them. The better the players, the better the leader. Few people are successful unless a lot of people want them to be. Andrew Carnegie said, "It marks a big step in your development when you come to realize that other people can help you do a better job than you could do alone."

Below is an illustration of what can happen to an organization when the key players slightly increase their potential while they work for the same team.

$$3 \times 3 \times 3 \times 3 \times 3 = \underline{243} + 25\% \text{ increase individually}$$
$$4 \times 4 \times 4 \times 4 \times 4 = \underline{1024} + 400\% \text{ increase together}$$

A great leader develops a team of people who increase production. The result? The leader's influence and effectiveness begin to multiply (working through others) instead of adding (working by oneself). That no man can sincerely try to help another without helping himself is, according to Ralph Waldo Emerson, one of the most beautiful compensations of this life.

David Jackson, founder and chief executive officer of Altos Computer Systems, said, "In my experience, the real turning point in a company is when you go from one to two people. Then, at least, there's someone to answer the phone while you eat your lunch."

All leaders have "war stories" of bad experiences in leading and developing staff. Perhaps this humorous illustration will help us laugh about our past experiences and allow us to get a second wind to begin building a winning team around us:

As nearly everyone knows, a leader has practically nothing to do except to decide what is to be done; tell somebody to do it; listen to reasons why it should not be done or why it should be done in a different way; follow up to see if the thing has been done; discover that it has not; inquire why; listen to excuses from the person who should have done it; follow up again to see if the thing has been done, only to discover that it has been done incorrectly; point out how it should have been done; conclude that as long as it has been done, it may as well be left where it is; wonder if it is not time to get rid of a person who cannot do a thing right; reflect that the person probably has a spouse and a large family, and any successor would be just as bad and maybe worse; consider how much simpler and better matters would be now if he had done it himself in the first place; reflect sadly that he could have done it right in twenty minutes, and, as things turned out, he has had to spend two days to find out why it has taken three weeks for somebody else to do it wrong.

In spite of all the problems that arise in the development of staff, two facts are certain. First, only as we develop a team do we continually succeed. A Chinese proverb says, "If you are planning for one year, grow rice. If you are planning for twenty years, grow trees. If you are planning for centuries, grow men." Second, only as we develop a team do we continually multiply.

A PICTURE OF A WINNING TEAM

Winning teams. . . .

- have great leaders
- pick good people
- play to win
- make other team members more successful
- keep improving

WINNING TEAMS HAVE GREAT LEADERS

Everything rises and falls on leadership. There are two ways you can get others to do what you want: You can compel them to do it, or you can persuade them. Compulsion is the method of slavery; persuasion is the method of free men.

Persuading requires an understanding of what makes people tick and what motivates them, that is, a knowledge of human nature. Great leaders possess that knowledge.

In a recent survey, seventy psychologists were asked: "What is the most essential thing for a supervisor to know about human nature?" Two-thirds said that motivation—an understanding of what makes people think, feel, and act as they do—is uppermost.

If you understand what motivates people, you have at your command the most powerful tool for dealing with them.

People Management has been studying the personal histories of tens of thousands of people since 1961. They found that, without exception, people repeat a pattern of behavior every time they accomplish something they think they do well and find deeply satisfying. They also found that excellent leaders underscore this behavior in the following ways.

Excellent Leaders Create the Right Environment

They believe in their team. This creates an environment for success. The best way to gain and hold the loyalty of your personnel is to show interest in and care for them by your words and actions. Sam Walton said, "Outstanding leaders go out of the way to boost the self-esteem of their personnel. If people believe in themselves, it's amazing what they can accomplish."

Excellent Leaders Know Basic Human Needs

Paul "Bear" Bryant, the legendary football coach at the University of Alabama, said there are five things winning team members need to know:

1. what is expected from each one;

2. that each will have an opportunity to perform;

3. how each one is getting along;

4. that guidance will be given where each needs it; and

5. that each will be rewarded according to his contribution.

Excellent Leaders Keep Control of the "Big 3"

Any leader who wants to play an active role in all areas of the organization may be tempted to take on too many responsibilities. However, three areas are crucial to the leader's authority and success:

1. **Finance:** because the finance staff is a prime means of exercising executive control in any organization.

2. **Personnel:** because the selection of people will determine the organization.

3. **Planning:** because the plan determines the future of the organization.

EXCELLENT LEADERS AVOID THE "SEVEN DEADLY SINS."

1. Trying to be liked rather than respected.

2. Not asking team members for advice and help.

3. Thwarting personal talent by emphasizing rules rather than skills.

4. Not keeping criticism constructive.

5. Not developing a sense of responsibility in team members.

6. Treating everyone the same way.

7. Failing to keep people informed.

T. Boone Pickens said, "There are many ways to avoid mistakes, but the best way to sidestep the disasters is to be available. You don't have to make every decision, but you should always be accessible. If your people are smart, they will keep you informed, and if you're informed, you're a part of the decision. With that in place, it's easy for you to back your people and that eliminates second guessing."

WINNING TEAMS PICK GOOD PEOPLE

When building the staff for his newly conceived computer company, H. Ross Perot hired the best people he could find. His motto is, "Eagles don't flock. You have to find them one at a time." He was saying that you can't build a strong team on weak individuals.

Adlai E. Stevenson said that there are only three rules of sound administrators: Pick good people, tell them not to cut corners, and back them to the limits. Picking good people is the most important.

Bobb Biehl says that from 60 to 80 percent of the success of any company or organization is attributable to three factors:

- a clear direction

- the right team of players

- sound finances

That's why few things are as important as putting the right people in the right places.

Recently I read a humorous article entitled "Who Not to Hire." It said never hire anyone. . .

- who is accompanied by his or her (a) slave, (b) attorney with a tape recorder, (c) bodyguard, (d) teddy bear, (e) police escort, (f) mother.

- who brags about being smarter than any three of the jerks he or she has worked for previously.

- whose résumé runs longer than forty pages.

- whose résumé is printed in crayon.

- who hisses at your questions.

- who occasionally lapses into pig latin.

- who breaks into wracking sobs when asked to name a personal reference.

- who is unable to decide hair and eye colors.

- who is, by court order, on permanent intravenous sedation.

- who tries to impress you with his or her repertoire of "knock knock" jokes.

- who, under salary requirements, scrawls, "I want it all now!"

While you're laughing, remember that Murphy's Law would seem to conclude that the ideal résumé will turn up one day after the position is filled! Still, getting the right people in the right places is crucial to the success of your organization. There are five principles for picking people that will help you get the best candidates on your team.

1. THE SMALLER THE ORGANIZATION, THE MORE IMPORTANT THE HIRING

Small organizations often make the mistake of thinking that they can get by with inferior staff members because they are small. The opposite is true. In a firm of one hundred employees, if one is inferior, the loss is only 1 percent. But if the organization has a payroll of two, and one is inferior, the loss is 50 percent. However, the bright side is that it's much easier to pick one excellent person than a hundred.

2. KNOW WHAT KIND OF PERSON YOU NEED (PERSONAL REQUIREMENTS)

Listed below are the "Top 20" personal requirements I look for in a potential staff member:

1. Positive attitude—the ability to see people and situations in a positive way.

*2. High energy level—strength and stamina to work hard and not wear down.

3. Personal warmth—a manner that draws people to them.

4. Integrity—trustworthy, good solid character, words and walk are consistent.

5. Responsible—always "comes through," no excuses; job delegated-job done.

6. Good self-image—feels good about self, others, and life.

*7. Mental horsepower—ability to keep learning as the job expands.

8. Leadership ability—has high influence over others.

9. Followership ability—willingness to submit, play team ball, and follow the leader.

*10. Absence of personal problems—personal, family, and business life are in order.

11. People skills—the ability to draw people and develop them.

12. Sense of humor—enjoys life, fails to take self too seriously.

*13. Resilience—able to "bounce back" when problems arise.

*14. Track record—has experience and success, hopefully in two or more situations.

15. Great desire—hungers for growth and personal development.

16. Self-discipline—willing to "pay the price" and handle success.

17. Creativity—ability to see solutions and fix problems.

---

18. Flexibility—not afraid of change; fluid; flows as the organization grows.

19. Sees "Big Picture"—able to look beyond personal interest and see the total picture.

*20. Intuitive—able to discern and sense a situation without tangible data.

*These things probably cannot be taught. The others can be taught with a proper mentor, environment, and willingness by the staff member. Most of the qualities in the above list can be evaluated with a couple of interviews and tests.

3. KNOW WHAT THE JOB REQUIRES

A job has certain characteristics that require specific skills and personality traits. These ten general questions will help a leader pick the right person. Does the job require . . .

1. an up-front or a behind-the-scenes person?

2. a generalist or a specialist?

3. a producer or a maintainer?

4. a people person or a paper person?

5. a leader or a supporter?

6. a veteran or a rookie?

7. a creative thinker or an abstract thinker?

8. constant supervision or little supervision?

9. a team player or an individual?

10. short-term commitment or long-term commitment?

The more you know about the kind of person you need and what the job requires, the greater your odds of hiring the right individual. Kurt Einstren says, "Hiring the wrong persons costs your company at least two years' salary. Many times there is a much higher price that is paid, not in cash, but strained relationships, bad PR, and lack of trust."

Often I am asked in leadership conferences, "How do you know which staff person to hire?" I always laugh and say, "You never know for sure," and my track record underscores that comment! These are some guidelines I have tried to follow when looking for staff:

- Know what you need before you start looking for someone.

- Take time to search the field.

- Call many references.

- Have several interviews.

- Include your associates in some of the interviews and ask for their input.

- Interview the candidates' spouses.

- Check out the candidates' track records.

- If possible, have a trial run to see if the job and the potential staff match.

- Ask hard questions, such as, "Why did you leave?"; "What can you contribute?"; "Are you willing to pay the price?"

- Trust your instincts.

There is only so much you can put on paper. If it looks good on paper but feels bad inside, go slowly. In fact, back off and let an associate take over; then compare conclusions. Personally, I only hire a person if it looks good *and* feels good.

4. KNOW WHAT THE POTENTIAL STAFF MEMBER WANTS

People work harder, stay longer, and do better on the job when they like what they do. Realizing this truth, I always make sure the potential team player feels good about me as the leader, the other players on the team, and the vision and requirements of the team. I always say to them, "Don't come unless it feels right." I know that no amount of money, attention, privileges, and promises will motivate a staff member who really does not want to be on the team. It is also important that the spouse "feels good" about the job. Positive feelings of a staff member will slowly disappear if the spouse is unhappy.

5. WHEN YOU CANNOT AFFORD TO HIRE THE BEST, HIRE THE YOUNG WHO ARE GOING TO BE THE BEST

Then:
Believe in them—that will encourage risk.
Show them—that will build respect.
Love them—that will strengthen relationships.
Know them—that will personalize development.
Teach them—that will enhance growth.
Trust them—that will develop loyalty.
Expand them—that will provide challenges.
Lift them—that will ensure results.

WINNING TEAMS PLAY TO WIN

The difference between playing to win and playing to not lose is the difference between success and mediocrity. I grew up in Ohio and became a fan of Big Ten football. Over the years I observed that Big Ten teams usually lost the "big game" every year at the Rose Bowl. Why? Were Pac Ten teams consistently better? No, the margin of victory was not a result of talent. It was a result of how each team approached the game. Big Ten teams played conservatively, trying not to lose. Pac Ten teams played wide open, trying to win.

Each time new staff members join our team, I give them each a plaque and ask them to display it on the wall of their offices. The words on the plaque read, "I don't have to survive." At the presentation, I encourage them to be not-survivors. I remind them to take risks, make tough decisions, live on the edge, and make a difference. People who play it safe continually miss opportunities and seldom make progress. It's the same way in baseball—you cannot steal second base with your foot on first! This is a favorite poem of mine. It describes those bland, safe people.

> There was a very cautious man
> Who never laughed or played.
> He never risked, he never tried,
> He never sang or prayed.
> And when he one day passed away,
> His insurance was denied.
> For since he never really lived,
> They claimed he never really died.

A recent survey of workers across the United States revealed that nearly 85 percent of those interviewed said they could work harder on the job. More than half claimed they could double their effectiveness "if they wanted to."[1] Winning teams are seldom more talented than losing teams. But they are always more committed. They want to win. They pay the price and go after victory. The crowd in the bleachers may wonder how they got so lucky, but the team members know they played to win.

WINNING TEAMS MAKE THEIR TEAM MEMBER MORE SUCCESSFUL

In other words, because of the other members of the team, each player is better than the player would be if he or she played alone. Vince Lombardi, one of the all-time great head coaches, said, "Start by teaching the fundamentals. A player's got to know the basics of the game and how to play his position. Next, keep him in line. That's discipline. The men have to play as a team, not as a bunch of individuals. . . Then you've got to care for one another. You've got to *love* each other . . . Most people call it team spirit."[2]

Robert W. Keidel said that trying to change individual and/or corporate behavior without addressing the larger organizational context is bound to disappoint. Sooner or later bureaucratic structures will consume even the most determined of collaborative processes. As Woody Allen once said, "The lion and the lamb may lie down together, but the lamb won't get much sleep."

What to do? Work on the lion as well as the lamb by designing teamwork into the organization. Although the Boston Celtics have won sixteen championships, they have never had the league's leading scorer and never paid a player based on his individual statistics. The Celtics understand that virtually every aspect of basketball requires close collaboration.

There are significant ways to engage in better team building.

KNOW THE KEY TO EACH PLAYER

Every individual has a personal agenda, the "real reason" he or she wants to be on the team. That personal agenda is the key to motivating each player.

MAP OUT A TEAM MISSION

Lay out the vision. Develop organizational mottoes, names, symbols, and slogans. This will encourage pride in team memberships.

DEFINE THE ROLE OF EACH PLAYER

This will help avoid unnecessary rivalries by clearly identifying each person's role within the group. This will also avoid the "fairness" issue that is common with staffs. Each player will be appreciated for his or her contribution to the team.

CREATE A GROUP IDENTITY

Establish your groups' worth by examining and promoting its history and values. Create memories together as a group.

USE LIBERAL DOSES OF "WE" AND "OUR"

Team building involves getting the members to feel a sense of ownership in what they are doing as a group. When the group has done well, it is important to praise the entire effort without singling out individuals.

COMMUNICATE WITH EVERYONE

Don't be a fact hog. Share information with everyone who is affected, not with just the key players. People are usually "down on" what they are not "up on." As a leader, you will know you have succeeded when the members of your team put the interests of the group over their own.

Do you recall when Edmund Hillary and his Sherpa guide, Tenzing, made their historic climb of Mount Everest? Coming down from the peak, Hillary suddenly lost his footing. Tenzing held the line taut and kept them both from falling by digging his axe into the ice. Later Tenzing refused any special credit for saving Hillary's life; he considered it a routine part of the job. As he put it, "Mountain climbers always help each other."

WINNING TEAMS KEEP IMPROVING

Whenever an organization is through improving, it's through! Why is it that a professional football, basketball, or baseball team seldom repeats as the world champion in consecutive years? Mainly, it's because of the temptation to keep all the players, practices, and strategies the same as the previous year. Too many think that if they "stay put," they can stay on top. That's not true. Either the current players must keep growing and improving, or potentially better ones must be brought into the organization. Continued success is a result of continued improvement.

The first objective of the leader is to develop people, not to dismiss them.

Studies have shown that day-to-day coaching, rather than comprehensive annual appraisals, is most effective for improving performance. This coaching process has two crucial components: setting specific objectives and holding frequent progress reviews.

Objectives should specify end results, the exact extent of achievement the manager expects, and should be tied to a timetable. How many objectives should the employee be given? In our experience, a few are better than too many. If the subordinate is overloaded, expecting all the objectives to be accomplished is unreasonable. Remember, the objectives are the primary measuring stick.

By *end results*, we mean what should be observably different as a result of the subordinate's performance on the job. All too often employees expect to be evaluated on the basis of how much effort they are putting into the job, rather than what they are accomplishing. This is especially true of weak performers. It is critical that the manager make clear that certain outcomes are expected and the subordinate will be held accountable for them. The manager should make every effort to set mutually acceptable goals. If there is disagreement, however, the manager must unhesitatingly insist upon setting the objectives. Remember: performance, not just effort, is the yardstick for meeting objectives.

Frequent progress reviews accomplish three things. First, they serve as a continual reminder that reaching the objectives is important to the person's career. Second, reviews give the manager a chance to recognize positive movement toward objectives. Third, if progress is not forthcoming, the manager can listen to the reasons for lack of performance and attempt to get the subordinate on track. The review becomes a problem-solving session.

Whether or not the employee makes progress, holding reviews permits the manager or boss to remain in control of the process.[3] If you have more than three people reporting to you right now, chances are you are unhappy with at least one of them. The situation usually has one or more of these elements:

- The person is not doing a top-notch job, but not a terrible one either; so you keep him or her around.

- Finding someone else who can do the job means interviewing, hiring (taking a risk), and then training the new person. You do not have time for that either.

- The person definitely is not doing the job, but you like him or her (or more likely you feel sorry for him or her).

- You don't quite have all the documentation you need to fire this person. Your last review was too flowery, and you have not really said how unhappy you are with the individual's work.

The result? Nothing happens. But keep in mind that you and the person who needs to be dismissed are not the only two people in the equation. What too many leaders fail to realize are the facts:

- The situation is well-known to other workers in the organization. No one can keep below-par performance a secret.

- Your failure to fire will have a detrimental effect on your career. As a leader, your first and greatest responsibility is to the organization and its highest good. Whenever a person's leadership position puts the personal agenda of himself or herself ahead of the organization, that leader is a liability.

- The morale of the other employees suffers because you keep the below-par performer on the payroll while everyone else is pulling more than enough weight.

Remember, it isn't the people you fire who make your life miserable; it's the ones you don't. If you have serious doubts about a staff member and have worked with him or her without success, it is better to have that person working somewhere else.

How can dismissing a person be handled correctly? Bobb Biehl says the essence of doing it right is in maintaining this perspective: "When you appropriately fire a person from a position in which he is failing, you are actually releasing him from that failure—and freeing him to seek a position in which he can find success. With a proper release, it's even possible to instill in a person the excitement that comes from anticipating a new adventure."

Obviously the optimum scenario is to interview well, hire well, and then begin to develop your staff to reach their—and your—greatest potential. There are three phases of potential:

1. I maximize my potential (I pour my energy into myself).

2. I maximize the potential of others (I pour my energy into key people).

3. They maximize my potential (they pour their energy into me).

Producers excel only at phase 1.
Leaders excel at phases 1 and 2.
Fortunate leaders excel at phases 1 and 2 and experience phase 3.

Let's take a moment now to stop and consider your strengths as a leader. This evaluation will allow you to review those areas of importance to a leader we've discussed in the pages of this book, while reinforcing the areas you need to emphasize in your development. Just circle the number that corresponds with how you see your ability, right now.

1	2	3	4	5
Mastered	Strong	Satisfactory	Needs growth	Difficult

Common Strengths Outstanding Leaders Share

DREAMING 1 2 3 4 5
Never let go of a dream until you're ready to wake up and make it happen.

In working with leaders, I have often asked myself, "Does the man make the dream, or does the dream make the man?" My conclusion: both are equally true.

GOAL SETTING 1 2 3 4 5
A goal is a dream with a deadline.

If you don't know what you want and where you are going, you will get next to nothing and end up nowhere.

INFLUENCING 1 2 3 4 5
The very essence of all power to influence lies in getting the other person to participate.

People do not care how much you know until they know how much you care.

PERSONAL ORGANIZATION 1 2 3 4 5
"Organizing is what you do before you do something, so that when you do it, it's not all mixed up."—Christopher Robin in *Winnie the Pooh*.

PRIORITIZING 1 2 3 4 5
"He is a wise man who wastes no energy on pursuits for which he is not fitted; and he is wiser still who, from among the things he can do well, chooses and resolutely follows the best."—William Gladstone

PROBLEM SOLVING 1 2 3 4 5
"The majority see the obstacles; the few see the objectives; history records the successes of the latter, while oblivion is the reward of the former."—Alfred Armand Montapert

RISK TAKING 1 2 3 4 5
Risks are not to be evaluated in terms of the probability of success, but in terms of the value of the goal.

DECISION MAKING 1 2 3 4 5
Your decisions will always be better if you do what is right for the organization rather than what is right for yourself.

CREATIVITY 1 2 3 4 5
There is always a better way . . . your challenge is to find it.

"Man's mind, once stretched by a new idea, never regains its original dimensions."—Oliver Wendall Holmes

HIRING/FIRING 1 2 3 4 5
"There are only three rules of sound administration: pick good [people], tell them not to cut corners, and back them to the limit. Picking good [people] is the most important."—Adlai E. Stevenson

"When you appropriately fire a person from a position in which he is failing, you are actually releasing him from that failure—and freeing him to seek a position in which he can find success."—Bobb Biehl

EVALUATION 1 2 3 4 5
People who reach their potential spend more time asking, "What am I doing well?" rather than "What am I doing wrong?"

The person who knows how will always have a job; but the person who knows why will always be the boss.

If you are strong in or if you have mastered four areas, you are on Level #1. If you are strong in or if you have mastered eight, you are on Level #2. If you are strong in or if you have mastered every area, you are on Level #3, and that means you have a strong support team that has allowed you to grow beyond yourself.

At this point in my life, I am fortunate to be living on the Level #3. I've grown beyond my own resources and am multiplying instead of adding because of those closest to me. I will be forever grateful to them. With them I will continue to lead. Because of them I will continue to grow.

Some of these precious people are:

Margaret Maxwell—my wife and best friend. Marrying her is the
    best decision I ever made.
Stephen F. Babby—my colleague and the wisest person I know.

Dick Peterson—my close friend, whose goal in life is to help me.

Dan Reiland—my executive pastor, whose loyalty and energy are unequaled.

Barbara Brumagin—my personal assistant, who has a servant's heart and superior skills.

Melvin Maxwell—my father, who is my hero in life and mentor in leadership.

EPILOGUE

This world needs leaders . . .

who use their influence at the right times for the right reasons;
who take a little greater share of the
blame and a little smaller share of the credit;
who lead themselves successfully before attempting
to lead others;
who continue to search for the best answer,
not the familiar one;
who add value to the people and organizations they lead;
who work for the benefit of others and not for personal gain;
who handle themselves with their heads and handle others
with their hearts;
who know the way, go the way, and
show the way;
who inspire and motivate rather than
intimidate and manipulate;
who live with people to know their
problems and live with God in order
to solve them;

> The growth and
> development
> of people is
> the highest
> calling of
> leadership.

who realize that their dispositions are
    more important than their positions;
who mold opinions instead of following opinion polls;
who understand that an institution is
    the reflection of their character;
who never place themselves above others except in carrying
    responsibilities;
who will be as honest in small things as
    in great things;
who discipline themselves so they will
    not be disciplined by others;
who encounter setbacks and turn them
    into comebacks;
who follow a moral compass that points
    in the right direction regardless of the trends.

NOTES

Introduction

1. David Hartley-Leonard, "Perspectives," *Newsweek*, 24 August 1987, 11.
2. Contributed by Doug Lysen, *Reader's Digest*, February 1989.
3. John W. Gardner, "The Nature of Leadership," Leadership Papers #1, Independent Sector, January 1986.
4. Richard Kerr for United Technologies Corp. *Bits and Pieces*, March 1990.

Chapter 1

1. James C. Georges, ParTraining Corp., Tucker, GA, interviewed in *Executive Communications*, January 1987.
2. J. R. Miller, *The Building of Character* (New Jersey: AMG Publishers, 1975).
3. Warren Bennis and Burt Nanus, *Leaders* (New York: Harper and Row, 1985), 222.
4. Robert Dilenschneider, *Power and Influence: Mastering the Art of Persuasion* (New York: Prentice Hall, 1990).
5. E. C. McKenzie, *Quips and Quotes* (Grand Rapids: Baker, 1980).

6. Fred Smith, *Learning to Lead* (Waco: Word, 1986), 117.

7. John C. Maxwell, *Be a People Person* (Wheaton: Victor, 1989).

CHAPTER 2

1. R. Earl Allen, *Let It Begin in Me* (Nashville: Broadman Press, 1985).

2. William H. Cook, *Success, Motivation and the Scriptures* (Nashville: Broadman, 1974).

CHAPTER 3

1. Dwight D. Eisenhower, *Great Quotes from Great Leaders*, ed. Peggy Anderson (Lombard: Great Quotations, 1989).

2. CCM *Communicator*, newsletter of the Council of Communication, Spring 1988.

3. Peter Drucker, *Management, Tasks, Responsibilities and Practices* (New York: Harper & Row, 1974).

4. *Newsweek*, 24 August 1987, 11.

5. Joseph Bailey, "Clues for Success in the President's Job," *Harvard Business Review*, 1983.

6. James M. Kouzes and Barry Z. Posner, *The Leadership Challenge* (San Francisco: Jossey-Bass, 1987).

CHAPTER 4

1. Quoted in Paul Wharton, *Stories and Parables for Preachers and Teachers* (Mahwah: Paulist, 1986).

2. Howard Hendricks, *Teaching to Change Lives* (Portland: Multnomah, 1987), 32.

3. Robert Lacy, *Ford: The Man and the Machine* (New York: Little Brown, 1986).

4. Bobb Biehl, *Increasing Your Leadership Confidence* (Sisters, OR: Questar Publishers, 1989).

5. Melvin E. Page and H. Leon Abrams Jr., *Your Body Is Your Doctor* (New Canaan: Keats, 1972).

6. John Maxwell, *The Winning Attitude* (San Bernardino: Here's Life, 1984).

7. Winifield Arn, *Growth Report No. 5, Ten Steps for Church Growth* (New York: Harper & Row, 1977).

8. George F. Trusell, *Helping Employees Cope with Change: A Manager's Guidebook* (Buffalo: PAT Publishers, 1988).

9. Bennis and Nanus, *Leaders*.

10. Trusell, *Helping Employees Cope with Change*.

11. R. F. Caldwell, "The Face of Corporate Culture," *Santa Clara Today*, November 1984, 12.

12. Max DePree, *Leadership Is an Art* (New York: Doubleday, 1989), 87.

13. Ron Jenson, ed., *Higher Ground*.

CHAPTER 5

1. F. F. Fournies, *Coaching for Improved Work Performance* (New York: Van Nostrand Reinhold, 1978).

2. Taken from a quotation by MacDonald in A. C. Remley, *Leaves of Gold*, (Williamsport: Coslett Publishing, 1948).

3. Adapted from G. W. Target, "The Window," in *The Window and Other Essays* (Mountain View: Pacific Press Publishing Association, 1973), 5–7.

4. Beihl, *Increasing Your Leadership Confidence*.

5. Tom Wujec, *Pumping Ions: Games and Exercises to Flex Your Mind* (New York: Doubleday, 1988).

6. John K. Clemens, *Hartwick Humanities in Management Report* (Oneonta: Hartwick Institute, 1989).

CHAPTER 6

1. Chuck Swindoll, *Improving Your Serve* (Waco: Word, 1981).

2. Nell Mohney, "Beliefs Can Influence Attitudes," *Kingsport Times News*, 25 July 1986, 4B.

3. Norman Vincent Peale, *Power of the Plus Factor* (New York: Fawcett, 1988).

4. Anonymous, "Attitude," *Bartlett's Familiar Quotations*, ed. Emily Morison Beck (Boston: Little Brown, 1980).

5. Viktor Frankl, "Youth in Search of Meaning," *Moral Development Foundations*, Donald M. Joy, ed. (Nashville: Abingdon, 1983).

6. C. S. Lewis, *Mere Christianity* (New York: Macmillan, 1952), 86.

7. Donald Robinson, "Mind Over Disease," *Reader's Digest*, March 1990.

CHAPTER 7

1. Thomas Peters and Robert Waterman, *In Search of Excellence* (New York: Warner, 1984), 58.

2. Frankl, "Youth in Search of Meaning."

3. Stephen Ash, " The Career Doctor," cited in Michigan Department of Social Services, *No-Name Newsletter*, Fall 1986.

4. Richard Huseman and John Hatfield, *Managing the Equity Factor* (New York: Houghton Mifflin, 1989).

5. Henry David Thoreau, *Bartlett's Familiar Quotations*.

6. Ron Watts, La Croix United Methodist Church, Cape Girardeau, MO, personal communication.

7. Huseman and Hatfield, *Managing the Equity Factor*.

CHAPTER 8

1. Robert K. Greenleaf, *The Servant as Leader* (Mahwah: Paulist, 1977).

2. Biehl, *Increasing Your Leadership Confidence*.

3. Quoted in "Weekend," *Newsday*, 8, 1990.

4. Harry C. McKown, *A Boy Grows Up* (New York: McGraw-Hill, 1985).

5. George S. Patton, *Great Quotes from Great Leaders*, Peggy Anderson, ed. (Lombard: Great Quotations, 1989).

6. Ralph Waldo Emerson, *Bartlett's Familiar Quotations*.

7. Roger von Oech, *A Kick in the Seat of the Pants* (San Francisco: HarperCollins, 1986).

8. Denis Waitley and Reni L. Witt, *The Joy of Working* (New York: Dodd, Mead & Co., 1985).

CHAPTER 9

1. Harry S. Truman, *Great Quotes from Great Leaders*.
2. Edwin Markham, *Great Quotes from Great Leaders*.
3. Edward Everett Hale, *Bartlett's Familiar Quotations*.
4. Stephen Covey, *The Seven Habits of Highly Effective People: Restoring the Character Ethic* (New York: Simon and Schuster, 1989).

CHAPTER 10

1. Huseman and Hatfield, *Managing the Equity Factor*.
2. Vince Lombardi, *Great Quotes from Great Leaders*.
3. William J. Morin and Lyle Yorks, *Dismissal* (San Diego: Harcourt Brace Jovanovich, 1990).

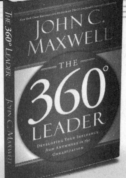